DAD AT L...

Read by all imp...

Personal dedications

TOUGH JOB: Dad-of-four first, Prime Minister second – Tony Blair picks up some tips from the first Dad At Large book

Acknowledgements

Production: **Richard Simpson**
Cover design and cartoons: **Steve Wetton**
Advertising: **Beryl Bell, Rowena Thompson**
Proof-reading: **Christopher Barron** (10p for each mistake spotted. His mum helped too – that'll cost me a lot more).
And **Buzz Lightyear** for giving me the idea for the title. Mind you, Buzz, the journey to vasectomy and beyond is far more hazardous than anything infinity has to offer.

Published by Newsquest (North-East) Ltd,
Priestgate, Darlington DL1 1NF
www.thisisthenortheast.co.uk/dadatlarge

Foreword

THE first Dad At Large book, which sold more copies than I ever dared imagine, ended with the birth of baby number four – a surprise, not a mistake.

Since then, all kinds of adventures have been survived, not least the dreaded vasectomy.

All those events, ordeals, laughs, disasters, and heartaches have been lovingly recorded in the Dad At Large column in The Northern Echo and brought together in this second book.

I owe a great deal to the thousands of people I have had the privilege to meet over the past three years as "The Dad At Large Roadshow" has taken me to wonderful places the length and the breadth of the North-East of England.

They have welcomed me, fed me far too well, listened to my talks, giggled in all the right places, and passed on a priceless collection of anecdotes from their own days as children, parents, and grandparents.

Many of those gems were published in the newspaper column and are told again in this book. To all those credited, and those whose names I've lost on misplaced scraps of paper, I thank you for your memories.

This second book is published with the support of Sure Start, Darlington. Sure Start is a cornerstone of the Government's drive to help disadvantaged children – aiming to improve the well-being of families and children.

And, since it is inspired by children, I am thrilled that each copy sold will raise money for The Butterwick Children's Hospice.

I hope it makes you smile along the way…

For family, friends and dads

For Christopher, Hannah, Jack and Max who make sure life is never dull! For Heather, who holds it all together, and my mum and dad for all their help and support. I love you all.
Also for dads everywhere. May they get the attention, rest and sympathy they deserve.
And in memory of Ian Weir, a much-missed dad, whose laughter can still be heard.

For every book sold, £1 goes to The Butterwick Children's Hospicewhich carries out such priceless work at Stockton

Peter Barron can be booked for speaking engagements on (01325) 505107. If you've heard him before, don't worry – there's plenty more where that came from! No personal fee is charged but donations can be made to The Butterwick Children's Hospice.

The things they say (about food)...

"DADDY, I love you almost as much as cheese sandwiches."
Still my favourite quote from my little girl Hannah after I'd read her a goodnight story a few years ago. It might not seem like very much to you, but I know how much she loves cheese sandwiches.

WE'D just driven past a restaurant specialising in Thai food.
"What's Thai food, Dad?" asked our eldest.
"Stupid – it's where you put knots in your spaghetti," replied his little brother.

STEPHEN Watson is 32 now, serves in the Navy and has three boys.
When he was ten and staying with his auntie Shirley in North Cowton, near Darlington, he was asked if he wanted some apple pie.
"Yes," he replied.
"What's the magic word?" asked his aunt.
"Abracadabra?" he suggested.

"YOU'VE taken one of my crisps...sob...it was the best crisp me ever had...sob...it was a funny shape...sob...me never get another crisp that funny shape again...sob" – Our Max, badly over-acting, after I pinched one of his crisps when he was two.

"CAN I have a lick of your lolly? I asked Max.
"No! This is a biting lolly not a licking lolly," he replied, sternly.

"I DON'T like these chips cos they're all chippy round my chops." – Max, aged three.

"Dad, come quick – one of the donuts Mum bought us is dead. There's blood pouring out of it into the box." – Max, aged four.

"GIANTS don't eat everything you know. For a start, they don't eat broccoli and you've got to respect them for that." Our Max, aged three.
(He's either picked it up from a video or he's destined to live his life on another planet.)

"MAX, eat your dinner and stop shouting at the table," said Mum.
"I wasn't shouting at the table I was shouting at Jack," replied Max, aged three.

And drink...

"DAD, is it right that we're not allowed upstairs with Coca Cola?" asked six-year-old Ben Blackwood, from Blackhall, County Durham.
"Aye, that's right," said his dad.
"That's all right then – this is cherryade," came the swift reply.

Second time around

ISN'T it funny how dads are treated like kids? Fatherhood, as I've remarked before, is simply childhood second time around.

The wheels turn full circle – and, in the most recent example, it's been bicycle wheels.

I remember, 20-odd years ago, asking my Mum and Dad for a bike: "No, you can't have one – we can't afford it, and you won't look after it properly," they said.

But there it was on Christmas morning – a lovely new bike, standing in the corner. Surprise, surprise.

I haven't had a new bike since and I've been asking for a one for months: "No you can't have one – we can't afford it, and you won't look after it properly," said my wife.

Our eldest – having just passed the latest childhood milestone of learning to ride without stabilisers – has just got a new bike for his seventh birthday. It's a mountain bike in luminous green. Very flash.

So when Father's Day arrived, I chanced my arm again: "If I had a new bike, we could go on rides together," I told him. (Using the kids to get your own way with Mum is always a useful tactic.)

But it was to no avail. Following a consultation in the kitchen, Mum insisted I couldn't have one and the kids all agreed. In fact, they seemed strangely eager to keep telling me I couldn't have one.

The birthday boy took particular delight in telling me: "You're not getting a bike for Father's Day Daddy, so don't expect one – and anyway, your bottom wouldn't fit on the saddle."

Father's Day duly arrived and I awoke to a number of home-made cards. The boy's had an anorexic horse and fat tennis racquet on the front and the following message inside: "Daddy, I love you so much it makes my hart brake."

There was no sign of anything in the way of presents but there was an awful lot of whispering and sniggering going on.

"Daddy, come down into the dining room but don't open your eyes," I was instructed.

Seven-year-old, five-year-old, three-year-old, and Mum with new baby in her arms led me into the dining room and I was told I could open my eyes.

There in the corner was a shiny new mountain bike – without stabilisers – all for me.

What a joy it's been to ride side by side with

the boy across the fields to watch the trains, splashing through puddles with our legs up, and flying down hills. It seems only yesterday that we were following the same path with me on foot and him strapped into a kiddie-carrier on my back.

But it's not all plain-sailing on bikes. I discovered how back-breaking it is to lift two bikes over stiles that crop up far too regularly – and I managed to fall into a bed of nettles during one particularly tricky manoeuvre.

But it's a small price to pay for being back in the saddle. And don't let on, but I knew I was going to get a new bike...

An ill wind...

A DAD who lives over the road from us didn't have such a fruitful Father's Day as me. He got a card from his little girl which said very innocently: **"DEAR DADDY – HAPPY FARTER'S DAY."**

A bad case of the Phoebe-jeebies

SOMEHOW, we'd got through the first seven years of parenthood without giving in to the kids' requests for a pet.

No cats, no dogs, no goldfish, no tortoises, no budgies. In the dim and distant past, there was Pickles – the one-winged butterfly the boy kept in a matchbox – but he didn't really count on the grounds that he was dead.

But then came the age of the 'cyberpets' and – stupidly – we gave in to the boy's pleading to join the craze that's sweeping the country.

Cyberpets, for the uninitiated, are little hand-held computers which come in the form of cats or dogs.

You have to feed them, clean them, take them for walks, play games with them and put them to bed.

Look after them and they live longer. Neglect them and they die or run away. They even 'cry' when they need attention. If it all sounds completely barmy, it is.

Anyway, the boy had £10 saved up from his birthday and he wanted a cyberpet kitten.

The lady at Woollies agreed to keep one aside for him and she was told that Daddy would be in before 10am to pick it up.

The boy was beside himself with excitement when I arrived back home with his very first pet: "I'm going to call you Phoebe," he said, activating the little computer after deciphering the instructions which had baffled his Dad.

Phoebe came to life. We fed her with milk and cat food. We emptied her litter tray. We played with her. The boy talked to her as if she was – well, real.

"I can't take her to school Dad, so you'll have to feed her and take her for walks at work," said the boy.

I have four children and a hectic job. I have enough on my plate without having to look after a computer cat but I did as I was told.

She 'cried' at work because she needed changing. Quite frankly, I felt like crying myself.

Not surprisingly, Phoebe didn't seem to be thriving. After a week, she still weighed only 1lb – her birth-weight. The boy was worried. So was I.

But then there was great excitement last Sunday morning while I was having my first lie-in for months.

"Daddy, Daddy, you won't believe this, it's Phoebe's birthday," the boy announced bouncing on the bed, Phoebe in hand. Phoebe had gone from 0-years-old to one-year-old and gained a pound.

Oh joy. Suddenly, the other kids were on the bed along with Mum, and we were all singing 'Happy Birthday' to a computer pet. Sadly, I wasn't dreaming.

But the next day, the happiness was replaced by tears.

Phoebe went missing. We searched in vain down backs of chairs, under beds, and anywhere else we could think of.

For two days, the boy fretted. So did I.

And then, on Tuesday night, the phone call came at work: "Daddy," said the boy, "it's terrible."

"What's terrible?" I asked.

By now, he was crying: "There's been a death in the family."

"Who's died?" I asked, more than a little alarmed.

"I can hardly say it, I'm so sad…it's, it's PHOEBE," he declared, breaking into full-scale sobs.

It transpired that she'd been found under the kitchen table.

Unloved, uncared for, she'd passed away. It might have been described as a cat-astrophe.

But the world of cyberpets is a miraculous one – dead ones can be reactivated.

And so it came to pass that 'Phoebe 2' was born yesterday and I really can't wait for her birthday.

Can anyone rescue me from this madness? **PLEASE!**

The cost of inflation

HOLIDAYS used to be relaxing. Often, they were boring. We'd spend a fortnight sitting on a beach, eating, drinking, and reading. Pretty dull really.

Take our honeymoon in Turkey. It was so hot you couldn't move, let alone do what you're supposed to do on honeymoon! The highlight was throwing pebbles into my wife's shoe while we sat on the beach, counting the days until we could come home.

Holidays are different now. With kids, they're certainly not relaxing – and they're anything but dull.

Somehow, we ended up spending the past two weeks with four kids in a caravan in Clacton. It was supposed to be a fortnight in France, but it went pear-shaped at the last minute and – after a frantic ringaround the holiday companies – Clacton's caravan was the only option at short notice.

We played on the beach every day but there was no time for reading. It was a case of: "Dad, come and have a look at my sand-castle...Dad, fetch buckets of water for my moat...Dad, I need a wee...Dad, can we go in the sea?...Dad, can we go on the pier?...Dad, can we have some chips?...Dad, can we have some candyfloss?...Dad, Dad, Dad, Dad, Dad, Dad."

I was up and down like a man with his tie caught in the lift door. Exhaustion quickly took over – and that was before the sorry episode with the inflatable dinghy.

"Can you blow our boat up Dad, can you, please Dad, can you?" (We'd bought it fully inflated at the start of the holiday but had to let the air out to get it into the car.)

Dads get all the best jobs so I puffed until I was dizzy – but the dinghy hardly swelled. I'd still be there now, trying to blow the blessed thing up, if my wife hadn't suggested taking it to a sea-front shop to ask if they could help.

"Do you have a machine to blow this up?" I asked the young girl serving.

"Cost ya a parnd," she replied. I think she meant a pound but they talk funny down there.

Thinking of my lungs, I readily agreed and the girl, fag in hand, attached a machine to do the business. As I took a well-earned rest, the dinghy bulged, and bulged, and bulged...and EXPLODED!

She'd blown it up too far: "It's burst," she said.

"I can see that," I replied.

"I've got a puncture repair kit out the back," she suggested.

"No, I'd like a new one please," I insisted.

Clearly deflated, she shouted Tracey, her boss, for advice.

Tracey, an Eastenders natural, duly appeared. "It's burst," she said upon expert investigation.

"I know," I said.

"Take it back where you gorrit and tell 'er there's an 'ole in it," she instructed.

"You burst it, you replace it," I demanded.

Tracey and her helper retreated out the back and could be heard arguing. Then the assistant returned with a sour look and thrust a new dinghy at me.

"Aren't you going to blow it up for a parnd then?" I asked politely.

"No, I'm bleedin' not," she huffed, looking away.

Back on the beach, the kids, sick of waiting for their Dad, were playing a game. They were throwing pebbles into their mum's shoe.

I've come back to work for a rest.

A hairy time at the health farm

HEALTH farms are meant to be relaxing places. Not in our house they're not.

It started when the full, horrific realisation dawned that I'm definitely going thin on top.

I can see more of my head every time I look in the mirror. I can't pass a shop window without seeing the patches of exposed flesh flashing at me through my hair like beacons on a hillside.

So, when an alleged cure for hair loss arrived in the office, I was volunteered to be the guinea pig despite the fact that there are several people around far more follicularly-challenged than me.

The 'cure' involved pouring stinging liquid from little vials onto my head twice a week. The fact that it made me go all blotchy where it had dripped down my body, was a cause of some concern but I pressed on.

"What are those red marks, Dad?" asked our eldest after one of my hair-restoring sessions.

"It's from the stuff that's supposed to stop me going bald but it stings a bit," I replied.

"Don't worry Dad, I've got just the thing to make your hair grow," the boy declared, running off to another room.

He returned with his little electric organ under his arm and started to plug it in. His little brother and sister were looking on as puzzled as me.

"This is what you need to make your hair come back Dad," he announced, "some warm and soothing music."

With that, he started playing an unidentifiable tune on his organ. Seconds later, his brother and sister were standing on chairs, looking down at my scalp, to see if it was having any effect.

"Keep going Christopher – it's working. His hair's growing," shouted his sister.

The boy played his keyboard more maniacally. I couldn't help wondering if this was how Bobby Crush started – perhaps his dad was as bald as a billiard ball.

But it didn't stop there: "Do you want to come to our health farm Dad?" asked the boy, who's always had an over-active imagination.

I was led by the hand into his bedroom and told to lie face down on the bed with just my shorts on. The boy proceeded to play his organ while his sister massaged my head, and their three-year-old brother went up and down my body, beating me with a hair-brush.

"It'll all help your blood flow better," said the boy knowledgeably.

Their Mum poked her head round the door to see what was going on and retreated in a fit of giggles.

It's all right for her – she's not going bald.

The things they say...

"DON'T worry, Dad – you're not going bald. It's just that your head's getting bigger." – Our Christopher a few years back. (My head's still getting bigger.)

Sad, bad and oh-so precious times

MY five-year-old daughter walked into the room. "Daddy something very sad has happened," she said.

"Princess Leia was being chased by the phogoggyphers and she got killed."

Even if she was getting her princesses mixed up (Leia is the one from Star Wars), it seems Princess Diana's death has touched everyone, no matter how young.

"But she's gone to heaven so she'll see Nanny (their grandma) up there, won't she and lend her her crown?"

We hadn't talked to the children about Diana's death, but our little girl had obviously picked up the news from listening to adult conversations. In truth, she wasn't too upset. To her, Diana was just a fairytale princess she'd seen on television. Real life, and the terrible sadness it often brings, remain blissfully distant.

On the first day back at school this week after the long summer holiday, the children in the playground were far too excited at seeing each other again to be unduly distracted by the tragedy which has so traumatised the nation.

The girls chatted in corners about new clothes while the boys ran around like lunatics, showing off embarrassingly, and jabbering away about the things they'd done on holiday.

"Have you ever been to Lightwater Valley?" said one. "Yeah, zillions of times," said another, before they both started running around crazily, pretending to be rollercoasters.

"My lunchbox is better than yours, cos it's got The Lost World on it," said the first. "Oh no it isn't, you big fat boaster," said the second.

Our eldest, who was starting at junior school this week, liked Diana best "because she cared for all the poor people".

His class chatted about what had happened to her for a while on the first morning back, but most of the talk when he got home was about Dennis the gerbil dying at lunchtime.

"It's sad when any living creature dies," he said, philosophically, before launching into a sword-fight to the death with his little brother.

After two days of national grieving, it was a relief to see that the children were largely unaffected. There's plenty of time for them to realise how hard life can be. But you couldn't help sensing that it was different for the grown-ups.

Hands up all those mums and dads who, at the end of their tether, had shouted out at some point last week: "I can't wait for next week and you lot go back to school!"

The familiar summer holiday war cry was certainly heard more than once in our madhouse of a four-children home. The holidays might only last six weeks but it seems like six months.

And yet, after the weekend's events, parents everywhere had been made to think again.

Of course, there was some relief at the children going back. Everyone needs a break.

But wasn't there also a heightened sense of family around the country?

Didn't we all look at those pictures of Diana at her happiest – laughing with her children as they splashed down a theme park water chute – and feel a particular sadness as parents?

The tragedy reminded us how much we should treasure the time we have with our children because it can be so quickly taken away.

And that's why, when the children went back to school, it wasn't quite such a relief as it might have been.

The things they say (about religion)...

CHILDREN at a Sunday school in Bishop Auckland were asked to draw a Biblical picture of the flight into Egypt.

The teacher picked up one completed picture and admired the illustration of Mary, Joseph and baby Jesus but wasn't sure about the inclusion of a strange little animal.

"What's that creature there?" she asked.

"It's a flea," said the child who'd drawn it.

"A flea? Why a flea?" asked the rather puzzled teacher.

The child gave a sigh and answered: "Because it says in the Bible 'take Mary and child and flea into Egypt.'"

THIS is a true story told to me by Linda Dodds, of Bishop Auckland. . .

When her son Paul was a little boy, he came home in a state of great excitement.

"Mum, mum, I've found a ball in the river," he said, breathlessly. "But it's got someone's name on it and I think I know him."

He showed his mum the ball, which had the name M. Evans written on it in thick, black ink.

"I think he goes to our school," he went on. "We say a prayer for him every morning in assembly."

"You say a prayer for him every morning?" queried his mum.

"Yeah," replied the boy innocently. "We say 'Our Father, who's Martin Evans, hallowed be thy name...'"

AT a Sunday School in Ingleton – a rural community near Darlington – the children were being taught the parable of the lost sheep.

"Why was Jesus so concerned about just one sheep going astray?" the teacher asked.

There was a long pause before one little lad, a farmer's son, replied knowingly: "It must have been the tup."

"I BELIEVE in the Holy Trinity – God, Jesus and Father Christmas." – Our Jack, aged five.

A FORMER teacher from Horden called Isobel, now 93, recalls how she was looking over the shoulder of a little girl who had drawn a nativity scene.

"What a beautiful picture," she said. "That's obviously the baby Jesus and is that Mary?"

"No," replied the young artist. "That's the baby-sitter – Mary's having a night out with God."

RACHEL, aged three, came home from Sunday school in Darlington, and was asked by her dad over lunch what she'd learned.

"Well, there was some men and Thomas was there and they were sat in a room and suddenly someone peed in the corner."

"What do you mean?" asked her dad, nearly choking on his Yorkshire pudding.

"They were all frightened and they did it again and the man peed in the corner again."

The man turned out to be Jesus and he'd appeared in the corner.

A CHILD overheard saying The Lord's Prayer at Harrowgate Hill Junior School in Darlington:

". . .Give us this day, our daily bread, and forgive us our trespasses, as we forgive those who trespass against us, and lead us not into Bank Top Station."

Sword-fighting a losing battle

WHAT is it about boys? All they seem to be interested in is fighting – mainly with swords, guns and dinosaurs.

You never see a little girl sword-fighting, blasting away with toy guns, or staging a velociraptor battle, do you?

Our boys, aged seven and nearly four, are always fighting. The eldest confided at bedtime the other night that he's made up his mind about what he wants to be when he grows up.

"I'm going to be a freedom fighter Dad, to free people in poor countries and make good use of all my swords," he whispered.

He certainly has lots of swords. I regularly get dragged into the boys' battles and, naturally, always end up dead.

Sword-fighting with a four-year-old is particularly hazardous because he's just reached groin-height and my precious nether regions – now just a few short weeks away from the dreaded date with the gelding knife – take a fair old battering.

Then there's guns. We set out with the sworn intention of not buying any toy guns, but a boy will make a gun out of anything – a stick, kitchen roll tube, bits of Lego, even one of my golf clubs.

As for dinosaurs, we've got enough to fill Jurassic Park ten times over – and they're always having fights.

The little'un is devoted to a velociraptor called "Velocy". That's the other thing about boys – they're not very inventive when it comes to pet names and nicknames so they just take the first bit and stick a 'y' on the end.

That's why there's so many goldfish around called Goldy and a whole generation of men known to their friends as Smithy, Jonesy and Wrighty. We've got a cuddly toy in our house called "Rabby" – guess what type of animal he is!

Anyway, I guess boys will be boys, and our boys are probably pretty normal. Except for one thing – I can't for the life of me get them interested in football.

I thought all boys loved football, but not ours. Their mates come round and reel off the names of favourite players and discuss the game they watched the night before.

Mine wouldn't know David Batty from Nora Batty. I'm not the sort to apply undue pressure, but I admit I've been a trifle disappointed that they've shown no sign of being footy fans.

But suddenly, this week has seen a heart-warming breakthrough.

There I was, watching the highlights of the England game and celebrating the opening goal, when I heard a little voice behind me: "That was a good header, Dad. Can we sit on the settee and eat crisps and watch the match together?"

"Course we can," I said as my little girl settled down to a four-goal thriller in her Barbie nightie...

• **CYBERPET UPDATE:** You may recall how Phoebe, the boy's computer kitten, died recently and the house was in mourning until she was miraculously regenerated.

Well, Phoebe has gone for good this time. She was left in the boy's pocket when he put his trousers in the wash.

Whizzed around the washing machine at microchip-bending speed, she was discovered making a funny whirring noise before conking out altogether.

Cyberpets are meant to teach kids how to look after real pets. The school gerbil – there's a good chance it'll be called Gerby – is coming to stay this weekend. Bet it's really looking forward to it...

So farewell then, Mr Fertile

LET'S get straight to the point. The very sharp point. This time next week, my Mister Fertile days will be over as a total stranger takes a knife to my unmentionables.

Four kids in seven years is quite enough thank you and everyone tells me the 'v-word' – I can't bring myself to say it – is the best option.

To be honest, I didn't have much option. When news leaked out that our fourth was on the way, the women in our village delivered a petition which suggested that I either got myself booked in for "a little operation" – or they'd do it for me with a sharp knife on the kitchen table.

"It'll only be a small job from what I've heard, arf, arf," they all say. (What makes it worse is they all think they're being original.)

Still it's no more than I deserve.

A few years back, a colleague confided to me that he was about to have the v-word.

But I'm no good with secrets and the next day posters went up around the office announcing his delicate little operation.

I particularly regret handing him a jar containing two pickled onions and saying: "Thought you might like to see what they'll look like afterwards."

Juvenile, I know. I shouldn't have done it and I'm sorry. Somehow, he's found out the date of my surgery (I wouldn't care, I've only confided in the readers of The Northern Echo) and he's walking round with an extremely smug look on his face. Revenge is a terrible thing.

My surgeon asked me during a recent consultancy if I wanted local or general anaesthetic.

I swiftly plumped for local because I'm scared of being put to sleep. With four kids, it's an unfamiliar sensation.

I was politely informed that I could only have a local if my...er...undercarriage was 'relaxed'.

Relaxed? How on earth could it be relaxed?

I wondered.

Anyway, after a quick examination, the doc cheerily announced: "I'm delighted to tell you you have a very relaxed undercarriage. That makes it easier – I won't have to dig so deep so a local will be fine."

"It might be relaxed now," I thought to myself, "but wait 'til you've got a knife in your hand and it'll be so stressed-out it'll be chain-smoking."

I was trying hard not to think about it yesterday when a survey, full of statistics about the dreaded v-word, landed on my desk.

• Only 11 per cent of men have had it done.
• 90 per cent say it's relatively pain-free.
• Nine out of ten men who've had it recommend it (Why does that phrase remind me of cat food?)
• 19 per cent reported improved sex lives. (Likely story.)
• 25 per cent of victims – sorry, patients – did it as a loving gesture to their partners.

Hold on, I don't need the v-word to prove my love. After all, I'm the one who went into Our Price at the weekend to buy my wife The Osmonds Greatest Hits for her birthday. Now that's real love.

It was so acutely embarrassing that I found myself saying to the assistant: "It isn't for me," as if I was buying an illegal substance or pornographic magazine.

The aforementioned survey coincides with an advertising campaign this week extolling the benefits of the snip.

Posters are going up nationwide and adverts will appear in magazines and on radio. So, no matter how hard I try to black it out, there'll be no hiding place.

My date with destiny is fixed. And, whatever happens, it can't possibly be as humiliating as buying a CD featuring Puppy Love and Long-Haired Lover From Liverpool.

Can it?

At the cutting edge

BELIEVE it or not, there are people out there – mainly mums – who think us dads have it easy. I wish they'd been in our house this week because I've been to hell and back.

Last week marked my dreaded date with the surgeon's knife. After four kids in seven years, I'd been sent for the 'v-word' (otherwise known as the snip). But before you have the v-word, you have to complete a little task by way of preparation. Without going into unnecessary detail, it involves a razor and you'd have to be double-jointed to manage it alone.

Embarrassing though it was, I had to call on the help of my dear wife. Reluctantly, she consented and we agreed to do 'it' after we'd got the kids to bed the night before the op.

But, you know how it is, we had a glass of wine for Dutch courage first. One glass led to another. In the end, she was far too tiddly to be trusted with anything sharp near my unmentionables so it was postponed until morning.

We settled down to watch TV. Guess what BBC1's film that night was? The Razor's Edge – I kid you not.

Having got the kids off to school the next morning, we again contemplated the little job in hand.

"What am I going to do with the baby?" my wife asked. The problem was solved by an extremely timely visit by one of her friends, Rose, who was duly recruited to hold the baby while we disappeared into the bathroom.

There was no real game plan, other than I'd take a bath and we'd take it from there. It was at that precise moment that the hot water chose to pack up (some problem with the boiler). So there I was, lying in a cold bath – feet up on the sides – while the woman who can't even manage to slice bread straight came at my undercarriage with a razor, giggling so much that her hand was shaking. And all the time, Rose, in the next room, could be heard falling around laughing as well.

It struck me that the v-word itself couldn't possibly be any worse than this. Upon arrival at Darlington Memorial Hospital, I was shown into a waiting room to sit with two other white-gowned 'victims', one of whom was shaking so much he could hardly hold his newspaper.

When my name was called, I was made to wear a hat that made me look like Ena Sharples and it was off to the operating theatre.

"Where's the surgeon?" I asked as I lay on the violently-rattling trolley, waiting for action.

"Feeding his guide dog," said the nurse who'd been assigned to keep up my spirits.

"Sometimes there's music playing while they operate," she added. "It was 'The First Cut Is The Deepest' last week."

Somehow, I survived. The treatment was first-class and – though I endured agonies that put childbirth into perspective – I didn't cry once. Over a cuppa and a biscuit in the recovery room I was looking forward to going home and being looked after for a few days. Fat chance – my wife arrived with bad news. An aunt had died in Ireland and she was flying straight off for the funeral.

Instead of being pampered, I had to look after the kids on my own for three whole days in a sympathy-free zone while hobbling around like John Wayne after a cattle drive.

I was so exhausted by the third day that I nodded off in the chair, only for our four-year-old to wake me up by jumping onto my lap, sending me howling round the house like someone with a blow torch in his trousers.

Then, down at the school gates, our little girl sent several mums into hysterics by announcing that "Daddy's walking funny 'cos he's had an operation on his tentacles."

Don't ever tell me dads have it easy.

The things they say (at school) . . .

A LITTLE boy in Darlington, who had moved to another class, was asked: "What's your new teacher like?"
"The same as the other one but with a different face," he replied.

A MUM, who wishes to remain nameless, recalls a time in her life when she was helping out part-time in the village pub. Her son came home from school with a kitbag and promptly told his mum: "You're supposed to stitch my name on it with white cotton but I told the teacher you wouldn't have time cos you're always in the pub."

A GIRL at George Dent Nursery School in Darlington was asked 30 years ago if she wanted some rice pudding for dessert.
"No," replied the infant.
"No what?" asked the teacher.
"No fear," came the reply.

A BOY at a school in Bishop Auckland was listening intently to a history lesson all about Hadrian's Wall.
"Miss," he said, "I've got an Uncle called Adrian and he's a brick-layer."

ONE small girl, who shall remain nameless, came home from school one day and asked her parents: "How do you spell ponce?"
Rather shocked, the parents demanded to know why she wanted to know.
"Because I'm writing a story and it starts 'One a ponce a time,'" came the reply.

DEREK Grocott, a teacher at Norton Comprehensive School, near Stockton, was marking a geography paper at home and began to chuckle when he got to a passage on mountain ranges.
A boy, who needs to concentrate harder on his spelling, had written the immortal line: "The penis is the backbone of England."

THIS next one comes from the Richmond Ladies Luncheon Club, told during the vote of thanks by a former teacher called Mary Hall.
Mary was deputy head at Elmfield Infants School in Newton Aycliffe 20-odd years ago. Assembly one morning was all about the wonders of nature and migration in particular.
"There's one bird which stays here for the winter," said the head teacher, Mrs Scripps. "Does anyone know which one it is?"
The hand of a four-year-old girl shot up: "I know Miss. It's the Robin Redbreast – and I know a poem about the Robin Readbreast my Dad taught me."
Delighted, Mrs Scripps invited the little girl to share her poem with her school-mates and she got to her feet:

"Little Robin Redbreast sat upon a thistle,
The little fellow pricked his arse,
It made the bugger whistle."

Rocker shocker with a happy ending

DESPITE my vain attempts to turn him into a footballer, my eldest son's ambitions remain firmly fixed on the world of showbusiness.

He attends acting classes every Saturday and is busily rehearsing for a modern version of The Complete Works of Shakespeare. He plays a punk rocker – don't ask me why, but he does.

Last Saturday, he burst into my bedroom and announced: "Dad, Dad, I forgot to tell you, it's the dress rehearsal today. I've got to go dressed as a punk."

I lay there, still half asleep, waiting for the news to sink in: "Tell me you're joking," I said.

"If I was joking dad, I'd have made you laugh wouldn't I?" he replied.

I glanced at the clock – it was an hour before he had to be there and one of those occasions when dads have to act quickly.

Within seconds, I'd leapt out of bed, got dressed and was hunting for the hair gel. The boy's hair was pulled into spikes, then coloured purple and pink with some spray left over from Hallowe'en.

The next task was to hunt down every safety pin in the house. They were stuck on to his torn T-shirt, along with a couple of chains I'd found.

Then, his Auntie Hazel, who was staying for the weekend, got to work with the make-up. By the time she'd finished, he looked like something from Nightmare On Elm Street, never mind Romeo and Juliet.

There was no way I was going into the front entrance of the local arts centre with him looking like that, so we sneaked in the back way. We were late, so the other kids were already in there, sitting on the floor.

We burst in and froze on the spot. The boy gasped. Not one other child was dressed-up. He'd got the wrong day.

It reminded me of that Christmas edition of Only Fools And Horses when Del Boy and Rodney burst into a supposed fancy dress party as Batman and Robin, only to discover it was a funeral wake.

Panic-stricken, the boy turned and fled, with me in pursuit. I found him crying in the corridor. "I can't go in there Dad, I'm too embarrassed. They'll all laugh at me."

I looked down at him with his hair, pins and make-up and couldn't for the life of me work out why he thought anyone would laugh at him.

There were three options: Do a runner, brave the ridicule, or have a quiet word with the teacher.

I chose the teacher. He came out to see the boy and played a blinder: "Oh, you look fantastic. How did you get your hair like that? And those safety pins. Wow! Come and show the others how they've got to look on the night?"

The tears vanished, the boy agreed to face his audience, and he emerged unscathed two hours later with a smile on his face.

"They all said I looked great, Dad," he said. "I'm a model punk."

He asked if we could have lunch in the arts centre for a treat and, after all the trauma, I didn't feel I could say no. So there I was, sitting at a table with a seven-year-old who looked like something from another planet.

"He doesn't usually look like that," I kept finding myself saying to people looking on. "It's just that he's in a play."

I bet Alan Shearer's dad never had this much trouble.

Losing the plot, big time

THE boy's showbusiness career has come on in leaps and bounds since he first joined the local drama group and played the tail of the hydra, the multi-headed monster from Greek mythology.

That was only a practice role, though he was a very good hydra's tail by all accounts. Last week, he made his proper stage debut as a punk Henry VII in a modern version of 'The Compleat Works of Shakespeare' at Darlington Arts Centre.

Naturally, as his proud dad, I had to be there to watch. Well, at least that was the plan.

But I hadn't taken account of the role dads always get landed with at the theatre – baby minder.

I'd got a taste of it a few days earlier when we'd taken our four kids – aged seven, five, four and seven months – to see Snow White On Ice at Newcastle Arena.

Before Snow White had even got her skates on, the baby started getting restless. You guessed it – I had to get him out of the way before anyone was disturbed.

Call me Dopey if you like, but I spent two long hours, walking around the corridors of the Arena, rocking a (very heavy) baby. Inside everyone was obviously feeling Happy. Me? I was more miserable than Grumpy with toothache.

It might have been a great show, but I saw so little of it that I'm not really in a position to judge.

Anyway, there we were a few days later, all excited about our boy getting a stage part in Shakespeare.

Although he was playing Henry VII, all he really had to do was run on and do an impression of Ravanelli celebrating scoring a goal and pulling his shirt over his head.

Don't ask me what Ravanelli's got to do with Henry VII but I never understood old Shakespeare, let alone modern Shakespeare.

Within minutes of the curtain going up, the baby started whingeing and Muggins had to launch into the Rocker Horror Show again. This time – with my son's big moment a far bigger attraction than Snow White – I stayed at the back of the theatre and strained my neck to see the action.

My poor old arms were dropping off but I gallantly fought the pain and waited for the boy's dramatic entrance.

It was then that the babe in arms spat his dummy out and it landed somewhere in the darkness.

He started to wail so another dummy – yours truly – had to go down on hands and knees, still cradling the baby, and search for the missing "doddy".

Sweating profusely, and with the baby blubbing away, I managed to grab an Opal Fruit, a ten pence piece and the ankle of an old lady who went "ooh".

Tragically, the dummy stayed hidden somewhere in the blackness. Never mind Shakespeare, it was more like a Carry On film.

By the time I got back to my feet, the boy thespian was leaving the stage to warm applause having done his bit.

"Did you think I was good, Dad?" he asked afterwards.

"Absolutely fantastic," I lied.

In fact, it was quite a performance all round…

Things they don't say...

"I REALLY like my brother. We have so much in common and it's great to have him around."

Moved to tears

THE kids had only ever known one home: 10 The Wayside, Hurworth, near Darlington. We'd moved in to the smallish bungalow as newly-weds ten years ago. It was perfect for the two of us – then, before we knew it, we had four kids.

A bigger house became essential. In fact, if it wasn't for my recent (very painful) vasectomy, we might have ended up needing a mansion.

But the kids – especially our eldest – weren't happy: "I won't see my friends. I'll have to run away like Lassie and find my way home," he sobbed.

He was placated with the promise that he could have a goldfish – his very first pet – to make up for losing his friends.

We spent the weeks leading up to the big move endlessly packing boxes. 'She who must be obeyed at all costs' gave me the kids' room to clear. That's the worst one to do because it comes complete with a mountain of toys.

After copious quantities of blood, sweat and tears had been spilled onto the carpet, the room was eventually piled high with boxes, packed with everything from Lego pieces to roller skates, from dinosaurs to cuddly rabbits, from a vast collection of swords to an equally vast collection of Barbies.

For a moment I thought I was hallucinating with exhaustion, but then I realised one of the boxes was talking to me: "Whirr, you are under my command – obey, obey, whirr."

In the confusion, I thought it was my wife still barking out the orders but then it dawned on me that the voice belonged to Megatron, the boy's robot.

I eventually tracked down the right box, gave it a thump and Megatron shut his gob, only for a mechanical frog to start croaking inside the same box.

Toy Story was happening for real in my own house! The frog stopped when it felt my boot and the day finally came for the move. (Rumour has it that they were planning a street party in The Wayside to celebrate the new-found peace and quiet.)

Everything seemed to be going fine until the removal men announced they didn't have a big enough van. They'd have to do it in two goes which would take twice as long.

"You've got a hell of a lot of stuff haven't you," said one of them.

"So would you if you had four kids and a wife with more belongings than the entire Queen's household," I replied under my breath.

When the time came to leave, the boy cried, said a tearful farewell to his bedroom, and hugged all the walls. The baby started howling, the other two kids started complaining that they were hungry, and my wife blamed me because the van wasn't big enough.

To speed things up, I volunteered to cram some of the smaller boxes into one car while mum and the kids travelled in another.

So there we were in convoy: a removal wagon crawling along in front, a car-full of whingeing kids in the middle, and me and my blood pressure bringing up the rear.

Half of everything we owned was in transit and the other half was back in the old house, with a new family about to move in.

As we went over a bump in the road, I heard a familiar voice from somewhere in the boot: "Whirr, you are under my command – obey, obey."

It's the first time I've ever sworn at a robot.

The one that (almost) got away

THE man from the pet shop is owed a public apology. He's probably had a nervous breakdown and it's all because I've moved house.

Let me explain...The kids were a bit upset at leaving our old house because they'd miss their friends.

"I'll never ever see my friends again and I'll have to run away like Lassie," sobbed our eldest.

We decided to smooth the path to our new home by finally giving in to his repeated requests for his first real pet. (This is not counting the assortment of cyberpets he's killed, or Pickles, the one-winged dead butterfly the boy used to keep in a matchbox a few years ago.)

No, this time the pets would be alive. We decided they could have a goldfish on the grounds that they don't make much of a mess, they don't bite, and don't need taking for walks on cold winter mornings.

And so it was that we ended up on Saturday morning at a pet shop in Darlington, surveying millions of fish in assorted tanks.

The four-year-old was the first to choose: "I'll have that big black one with boggly eyes and a mouth going like this," he said, doing a fish impression.

The pet shop owner, by now armed with a net, went about his business and the big, black boggly one was quickly peering out of a plastic bag.

His sister, aged five, went next. She selected a white one which proved a little bit more elusive but not too difficult to catch.

Then came the eldest, aged seven. He'd decided in advance his would be called Arrow so it had to be small and fast, with a gold body and pointed white head.

He finally found one among the tanks which fitted the description perfectly. "That one please," he instructed the pet shop owner.

Arrow was, indeed, small and fast. He dodged this way, he darted that way. The pet shop man, calm at first, started thrashing around more and more frantically with his net but was getting nowhere.

In the end, he got fed up and caught another one which looked not too dissimilar. "Gotcha!" he lied. "There you go, son." The boy shook his head. "That's the wrong one," he said.

The pet shop man, none too happy, went back to the hunt. Beads of sweat were breaking out on his forehead, his net had stirred up whirlpools inside the tank and hundreds of fish must have been feeling distinctly dizzy before Arrow was finally in the bag.

The big, black, boggly one was duly named Bow (to go with Arrow) and the white one was called Emma.

Having bought a tank, gravel, food and a few weeds, we were all set to take the fishy trio home.

"Hang on, Dad," said the eldest, "I think I've just seen one that looks even more like an arrow."

We were ushered out of that pet shop faster than an arrow from a bow...

The things they say (about sex)...

A LITTLE boy from Darlington, who must remain nameless for obvious reasons, had come across the word 'penis' and asked his grandma what it meant.

"Well, it's another word for a willy," explained his red-faced grandma, as delicately as she could.

"Urghh," replied the boy. "That's the last time I eat any of those penis butter sandwiches."

"DAD, I know how babies are made – do you want me to tell you?" asked my six-year-old daughter.

"Well, what happens is that the daddy shoots out lots of seeds and they float down a tunnel looking for the mummy's eggs and then one of the seeds bangs its head really hard against the egg until it lets it in."

Then, after a pause, she added thoughtfully: "You must have had lots of seeds with hard heads to make all of us."

SANDRA Cooper, a midwife at the Friarage Hospital in Northallerton – birthplace of the Dad At Large kids – was eight when she asked her Mum the question all parents dread: "Where do I come from?"

"Ask your father," said her mum.

The flustered dad had kept a magazine showing a baby's birth and did his best to overcome his embarrassment and answer his daughter's detailed questions.

"Why did you want to know?" he asked, once his ordeal was over.

"Because my friend came from London and I just wondered where I came from," replied the midwife-to-be.

DENIS Bell, of Redcar, told me how his four-year-old grand-daughter, Jenny, was having trouble coming to terms with the fact that her mum was expecting a new baby:

"Where do babies come from?" asked Jenny.

"They come from Mummy's tummy," said her mum.

"Oh, is the pram in there as well?" came the reply.

SUZANNE Watson, of North Cowton, was only small when her mum was expecting another baby.

"Would you like a baby brother or sister?" she was asked.

"I'd rather have a pony," she replied.

Suzanne is 29 now and she's only just told her mum that she looked out of her window on every birthday to see if there was a pony in the field. There never was.

SUE Patterson, from Great Ayton, recalled the day her son Gary was sitting in the garden in deep discussion with half a dozen of his mates.

Suddenly, he ran inside to ask: "Mum how old are you?"

"22 son," she lied instinctively.

Gary ran back outside where his mum overheard him say: "Well, that's nothing – my Mum was only 13 when she had me."

"I'D like Mummy to have another baby but she can't because she's been spayed." – Hannah Heathman, aged eight.

Off to the great goldfish bowl in the sky

WHO told me goldfish were easy? "Get them some fish," they said. "They don't make any mess and they don't need walks on cold winter mornings."

So, we got the kids a goldfish each, a big, black boggly-eyed one called Bow, a pointy-headed gold one called Arrow, and an all-white one called Emma.

The novelty wore off after the first week and, naturally, I got the job of changing their water every Sunday. There was one small problem – I discovered I'm scared of them.

Nervously and dreading feeling them wriggle, I tried in vain to catch them in a glass, a jar, and then a small saucepan. I ended up using the tea-strainer and flicking them into the washing up bowl.

Anyway, it is my sad duty to report that we only have two of them now. You see, it's been a tragic week in the madhouse.

It started when the telephone rang at work just as an important meeting was about to begin. It was one of those calls which sends a shiver down the spine: "Daddy, something terrible has happened," sobbed my little boy. "There's been a death in the family."

My blood froze as I thought of all the loved ones who might have passed away. But thankfully, it wasn't my mum, dad, or either of my brothers.

"It's Arrow, Daddy. My goldfish – he's dead."

The relief was tinged with shock. Arrow had only been with us for three brief weeks. The boy, aged seven, had come down in the morning to feed the fish and there was poor old Arrow, floating motionless on the surface. He couldn't stop crying down the phone.

"Don't worry son, I'll get you another one," I said gently, but it just made him worse. "Never, never, never. Arrow was the best goldfish in the whole world," he blurted out.

He'd hardly paid the blessed thing any attention after the first couple of days, but death makes us wear rose-tinted spectacles.

Mum, being the squeamish type, hadn't been able to remove the body from the tank and had to rely on the boy's four-year-old brother to scoop it out and put it in a matchbox.

"It's all right Mum, I don't mind. I'll get the others out when they die as well," said the little 'un.

Mum was in a big rush to get the kids off to school so Arrow was left in the matchbox in the sideboard. Imagine what a terrible shock I'd have had if I'd come home and gone to light the fire with matches.

A couple of caring colleagues suggested ways of easing the pain for the boy.

"Just put the fish back in the tank and stir the water round with your finger really fast and it'll look like it's swimming," said one.

"What you should do is cut a carrot into the shape of a fish and say it's come back to life – he'll never know the difference," said another.

I couldn't help feeling slightly offended at the idea that my kids couldn't tell the difference between a goldfish and a carrot.

The funeral in the garden was postponed until I got home. We stood in a circle as Arrow – still in his matchbox coffin – was placed in a hole by a rose bush and covered with earth. The boy said The Lord's Prayer and marked the spot with a few wild flowers he'd picked.

We went inside and had a cup of tea. I couldn't help thinking it tasted a bit funny.

There were five in the bed

AFTER years of bed-hopping, we've finally got a king-size bed. In fact it's even bigger than king-size – it's a splendid six-footer. Oh, it cost a fortune, but when you've got four kids, you need a big bed.

This one's so big it took the delivery men an hour to get it up the stairs – and then they had to have a cup of tea to revive them.

But we were convinced it would all be worth it. Even if the kids did come in for a snuggle, there'd be bags of room for us all. It's so big, you could get a juvenile jazz band in it.

So there we were, just the two of us, on our first night in the new bed, enjoying acres of room. I drifted off to sleep, content in the knowledge that I wouldn't get squeezed out into the top bunk, bottom bunk, spare room or wherever else.

It was just after midnight when the baby woke up and came in with us. No problem, bags of room. At 2.30am, our four-year-old followed him. At 3.15am their seven-year-old big brother – he'd had a bad dream – joined in. Only our little girl remained in her own bed.

The alarm clock showed it was just after 4am when I woke to find myself on the very edge. The four-year-old was lying lengthways across my pillow, the seven-year-old had his legs over my stomach, the baby was attached to him like a little limpet, and Mum was cuddled up next to him. **AND SHE WAS DRIBBLING!**

We had this six-foot bed and we were all squashed up like sardines. I gave up and staggered off to the bottom bunk...

And it is probably a direct consequence of my general lack of sleep that I made a complete fool of myself the next day. I was in our village shop – brain-dead after the night before – when a man I vaguely recognised came up and said: "Now then, howya doing?"

It was one of those horrible moments when you are desperately trying to remember where you know someone from: "Oh hello there. I'm fine thanks, how are you?"

It got worse: "I'll be in touch soon about that little job," he went on, mysteriously.

"What job?" I said, desperately confused.

"You know – Paddy O'Doyle," he replied.

By now I was completely bemused but far too embarrassed to admit it: "Oh, of course. Yeah, just give me a ring any time," I babbled.

I walked out of the shop and drove home wondering who on earth the mystery man was: "Paddy O'Doyle, Paddy O'Doyle. I know him from somewhere," I said to myself repeatedly.

When I arrived home, I told my wife what had happened: "There was this fella in the shop who knows me called Paddy O'Doyle but I haven't got a clue who he is. He says he's going to be in touch about a little job."

"What did he look like?" she asked and I gave her his description.

"You idiot," she smirked. "It's the bloke who's going to do our PATIO DOORS!"

Well, it sounded like Paddy O'Doyle to me...

FISH UPDATE: It was my sad duty last time to report on the demise of Arrow, our eldest boy's pet goldfish. Well, there's more bad news on that front.

Emma, our little girl's all-white fish, has also gone to that great goldfish bowl in the sky. Another matchbox, another garden funeral, more tears. That only leaves Bow – and he's got an ugly-looking growth on his mouth.

Three weeks ago we had three healthy fish. Now all we're left with is the big, black, boggly-eyed one with a fat lip. Help!

And then there were none

JUST in case anyone from the RSPCA is reading this, I make this pledge here and now – there will be no more pets in our house.

Pets have become a decidedly dodgy subject. Let me recap briefly.

Back in September 1994, I was writing about Pickles, the one-winged butterfly. Our eldest – just four at the time – had found Pickles and kept him for weeks in a matchbox, feeding him leaves even though he was as dead as a dodo.

A year or so later, we were having a holiday at the in-laws down south and I'd been ill because of an allergic reaction to their cats.

To escape the cat hair, we'd gone for a day out in the New Forest and hired bikes. Mum had a bike to herself but I had to have one of those little chariots attached to mine, with two kids being carried along like Lord and Lady Muck.

It's bloomin' hard work pulling two kids behind you on a push bike, especially when you're going uphill, and I was on the point of exhaustion and sweating buckets as I pedalled towards the top of one particularly steep slope.

It was then that I heard a little voice behind me say: "Do you realise Hannah, if Daddy dies now we'll be able to get a cat."

We managed to avoid cats and all other animals until June 1997, when Paddy, the school guinea pig came home for the weekend. The only trouble was, no one told me. So when I heard a noise in the middle of the night, I crept downstairs, ready to confront a burglar, only to stub my toe on Paddy's cage in the darkness.

By the summer of 1997, we'd reached the age of cyberpets, and we managed to kill ours because the boy left it in his pocket when his trousers went through the washing machine.

And that brings us to the fish. Regular readers will know that a month ago, we finally succumbed to the kids' requests for a proper pet and allowed them to have a goldfish each. Bow, Arrow and Emma were duly bought from the local pet shop and installed in a tank in the hall.

It has already been my sad duty to report the tragic deaths of Arrow and Emma, both of whom were given decent matchbox burials in the garden.

Now, I have to own up publicly to the fact that we've managed to kill three fish in just a few weeks. Yes, Bow – the big, black, boggly-eyed one with a fat lip – has died from the same fishy infection which killed the other two.

Once again, our four-year-old volunteered to scoop out the body and put it in a matchbox, ready for the funeral. The trouble is that, after three dead fish, the novelty wore off, and Bow was left in his matchbox coffin on the garden table for a week without being buried.

It was only when we heard a terrible wailing sound coming from the garden that we realised something had gone badly wrong.

We looked out of the window to see, to our horror, that Bow's matchbox coffin had been torn to shreds on the lawn. And nearby, next door's cat was being violently ill. He'd obviously sniffed the fishy smell, gobbled Bow up, then made the painful discovery that a week-old dead fish with an infected lip is none too appetising.

So there we are – we're not only jinxed with our own pets, but we've made a start on killing other people's.

Anyone want to buy a fish tank?

Out of the mouths of babes

EVEN when you're on to child number four, the novelty of hearing your offspring's first words never fades.

With each of our children, we've waited with growing anticipation for the first intelligible utterance and jumped with excitement when it came. "I'm sure he/she has just said *Mummy*," my wife has squealed, with all of our first three kids.

The first word can never be *Daddy*, can it? I swear I'd heard at least one of them say *Daddy* before *Mummy* – but 'she who must be obeyed' would never have it.

In fact, this lack of recognition has been one of the great disappointments of fatherhood for me, along with the fact that my two older boys – aged seven and four – haven't shown the slightest interest in football.

But suddenly, all the years of feeling inadequate have been erased by our fourth baby who is rapidly approaching his first birthday.

Baby Max (it was his Mum's idea, I hate it – reminds me of Bygraves, Wall and Headroom) has just come out with his first words and I am beside myself with excitement.

It wasn't *Mummy* – or *Daddy*. Guess what? It was *Kick* followed by *Goal* while he was playing with a football in the lounge.

Eureka! After all these years, I've finally produced a child who's a football natural.

Well, he's bound to play for England, isn't he, if his first words are *Kick* and *Goal*? It stands to reason.

Okay, so it sounded more like *Gick* and *Coal*, but it's close enough.

My wife, who hates football more than I hate housework, is none too happy.

"I'm sure he said *Mummy* the other day," she said, though it's nothing more than the mad ramblings of a desperate woman.

But while I've been doing laps of honour round the house at this wonderful development in my life, we've also had reason to rue the day our eldest ever learned to talk.

You see, when you've got four kids aged seven and under, you don't get a lot of time for romance, so Mum and I had sneaked off upstairs for a...let's call it "an intimate moment" on a Sunday afternoon.

After a couple of minutes the telephone rang and all we heard was the boy pick up the receiver and say: "No, I'm sorry, Mummy and Daddy have popped upstairs for a cuddle and they told us to stay downstairs and watch a video."

The moment was lost. And until this day I've no idea who it was. It could have been a W.I. or a church group wanting to book a Dad at Large talk.

It could have been my boss, which would have been very embarassing. But my biggest fear is that it might have been my Mum, because she doesn't think we do things like that, my Mum.

The things they say (about animals)...

GEORGIA Turnock, aged three at the time, was told by mum Heather: "I'm sick of pandering to your whims."

"We haven't got a panda," replied Georgia, of Darlington.

PEOPLE have some strange pets – but I bet you don't know many who have a giraffe. Patrick, the three-year-old son of a friend, was telling us about the giraffe in his garden just the other day.

"A giraffe?" my wife asked. "Have you seen it?"

"No," he replied.

"Well, how do you know you have a giraffe in your garden?" she enquired.

"Because," he explained, "Mummy says 'Keep the doors closed or you'll let the giraffe in.'"

"WE'VE got to come in now cos Dad's been bitten by midgets." – David Malcolm, aged seven, from Middleton St George, near Darlington. The family were on holiday at the time – at Diddyland presumably.

DAVID'S sister Becky, nine, had her mum expecting the worst as they drove to pick up the school gerbils for the summer holidays.

"I know the difference between boy gerbils and girl gerbils," she said.

"Oh really?" ventured her mum.

"Boy gerbils get the big water container and girl gerbils get the little one," replied Becky.

IT'S not for me to cast doubt on the drawing abilities of Brown Owl at our local Brownie pack. But she *was* responsible for the colourful home-made chart of common garden birds which our little girl brought home recently.

The chart has been pinned to the window facing the back garden so Hannah can tick off the birds as she spots them.

Her little brother has taken a keen interest too: "Hope we spot one of those parrots soon," said Jack, pointing to a blue tit.

MAX, aged three, was enjoying a sight-seeing ride in his seat on the back of my bike.

"Look Dad," he shouted, "there's a dog poo in the road".

"No, it's not a dog poo, it's a horse poo," I shouted back.

"No, it's not a horse poo – it's a dog with an eno-o-o-ormous bottom."

VIRGINIA Watson, of Carlton, near Stockton, was only two when her mum Pauline was brushing her teeth one night:

"It's really important to remember to brush your teeth," her mum told her.

"Oh, I do Mum," replied the little girl. "And I brush Max's teeth."

Since Max was the family dachshund, her mum was not unnaturally a little alarmed:

"You brush Max's teeth?"

"Yes, every night," replied Virginia.

"And what do you brush Max's teeth with?" asked her mum.

Virginia pointed to the brown toothbrush which belonged to her dad Theo.

The little girl is grown-up now. It was another 30 years before her dad was finally let in on the ghastly secret.

Confessions of a disco dad

DECADES have passed since I'd last been dragged along to a school disco.

I didn't dance. The boys didn't. We just hung around the walls trying to look cool, wrestled a bit and ran around aimlessly.

I remember the records even now: Tiger Feet, Do Ya Wanna Be In My Gang and the immortal Remember You're A Womble.

Twenty years on, there I was, preparing for my first school disco as a dad. My seven-year-old son came downstairs in his best crimson waistcoat and black trousers. (Mercifully, the days are gone when he went to discos in his Thunderbirds hat.)

My five-year-old daughter wore purple trousers with a green top. She'd had her hair carefully plaited and was wearing it in bunches.

"Can you take the kids to the disco?" my wife asked. "Juliette's dad is going."

"What's he wearing?" I demanded to know.

I was wearing my burgundy shirt, blue jeans and brown leather jacket. Juliette's dad promised not to clash when I telephoned.

"You look nice," he said when we arrived.

"You too," I replied. "Want an orange juice?" We hung around the walls with a few other dads, trying to look cool, but resisting the temptation to wrestle.

"You'll have to dance you know," said a mum on the organising committee. The Birdie Song was playing. "Yeah, in a minute," I promised.

"I wish they'd play some All Saints songs," said Juliette's dad.

"I like the Spice Girls," added Natalie's dad, who started humming 'Wannabe' before he realised what he was doing.

"I like that Robbie Williams one about Angels," I chipped in to save his blushes.

"Anyone want another orange juice?" asked Juliette's dad.

Meanwhile, the disco was in full swing. Girls at school discos look ten years older than they really are: mini skirts, make-up, hairdos, raunchy dance moves.

Time hasn't changed the boys; 99 per cent of them still don't dance. They play a game which must be called: Who can be the most stupid? This involves a number of activities: 1. Wrestling 2. Talking very loudly in a vain attempt to attract the attention of girls. 3. Going to the toilet a lot so they have something to do. 4. Running around and sliding across the floor on their knees.

The one per cent of boys who break ranks have a simple philosophy: "If you're gonna dance, the only cool way is to do it as stupidly as possible."

I thought one boy was having a fit at first. His arms, legs and head went in all directions before he did the obligatory bottom-swivel. He undoubtedly has a future in farming as a threshing machine.

The Spice Girls came and went. Robbie, sadly, stayed in the CD box. (45s mean nothing to today's kids.)

Then, right near the end, they played a new souped-up version of a song which has apparently returned to the hit parade after 20 years. The familiar strains of Remember You're A Womble filled the hall.

I felt my bottom wiggle just a touch. Then I remembered I was a dad, not a Womble, and asked Juliette's dad if he fancied another orange juice.

The Max factor

DURING a recent talk to the Durham County Federation of Women's Institutes, I was reflecting on how much I hate our baby's name Max because it reminds me of Max Bygraves.

The federation has kindly written with some startling news: "We've discovered that Max Bygraves' real name is Wally. It could have been worse," the letter said.

All I need now is for it to be revealed that Max Wall was really called Dick and my life will be complete.

The whole tooth and nothing but the tooth

THE boy's two front teeth had been wobbling for weeks. He insisted, with some irritation, that he hadn't been kissing the girls. (I hated it when my dad asked me that question too.)

Suddenly, within days of each other, the gnashers finally fell out, leaving him looking like a cross between The Son of Dracula and Albert Steptoe.

"I have to write a letter to the tooth fairy straight away," the boy announced excitedly.

"Me too," said his little sister.

We've had visits from the tooth fairy before, but this was the first time she'd received correspondence. The boy's read thus:

"Dear Tooth Fairy, all I've wrote this for is to tell you that I'd like to know why you don't let humens see you? Christopher (the boy who lost his tooth)."

His sister's letter had lots of hearts, kisses and tulips drawn on and said: "Dear Tooth Fairy, I just want to now wot you wear."

When they were finally asleep, the tooth fairy flew into their room and left two 50 pences under the boy's pillow.

The tooth fairy also left both the boy and his sister a letter each in reply. The answer to the boy's question was that she flies too quickly for 'humens' to see her and she has to stay invisible because some naughty people want to trap fairies. The answer to his sister was that she wears 'a very light rainbow-coloured dress and little soft shoes'. In cold countries, she also wears a 'fluffy, warm cardigan and bonnet'.

(Actually, the letters weren't written by the tooth fairy. They were written by me – but please don't tell anyone I'm a fairy.)

For someone who's just hit 35, my own teeth aren't doing too badly.

But, while the boy has been getting more and more concerned about his tootsy-pegs falling out, I've been getting anxious about my hair falling out. I needn't have worried – the kids have come up with the answer.

A character called 'Mister Spud' joined the family recently. The kids simply had to stand him in a saucer of water for a few weeks and watch his hair grow like magic. Well, it's actually grass which sprouts from a potato head, but we won't split hairs.

"Maybe if you stand in a bath of water for a while, you won't go bald Daddy," suggested my four-year-old, helpfully.

The question is: Do I really want green hair?

The things they do...

When the Dad At Large speaking tour hit the lovely County Durham village of Redworth, I had the pleasure to meet a jovial chap called Jim McMillan. He's 58-years-old now, but having listened to some of the things my kids get up to, he was eager to pass on a delightful episode from his own childhood.

He went on to tell me how, when he was about five, he'd had to collect and press wild flowers in his school book. There was an annual prize for the best collection of pressed wild flowers and Jim won it every year.

"We used to have three aunties came to tea every Sunday," he explained. "They were all, ya know, stout women."

"Do you mean fat?" I enquired.

"Aye, if yer like," he replied. "Anyhow, they were reet big. All I had to do was put me book under the settee cushion every Sunday and I had the best pressed flowers in County Durham."

Help! My wife is having an affair

IN a few weeks, it will be our tenth wedding anniversary. It should be a time for romance – time to celebrate a marriage which has borne four wonderful children.

Instead, I am a devastated man. Why? Because my wife – she who vowed to love me till death do us part – is having an affair. Yes, a passionate, obsessive, all-consuming affair.

The object of her attention is on the small side and kind of artificial in my eyes.

But he's smooth, exciting, modern and totally responsive to her needs. She can't keep her hands off him.

He came into our lives at Christmas. His name? 'Game Boy'. You know the sort – one of those hand-held computers with games attached.

Our seven-year-old had asked Santa to bring him one, then slept with his fingers crossed all night in the hope that he'd find one in his sleigh.

Well, Santa found one all right, but the boy doesn't get to play with it anywhere near as much as his mum.

I come home from work and there she is – sitting on the settee playing with him. Caressing him, talking to him, making noises of ecstasy when he does something she likes. She even takes him in the bath with her. I can hear him bleeping while she splashes her legs in excitement.

There was a household crisis a week ago when the baby picked up Game Boy and threw him in the bath water.

You should have seen the panic – mum dropped everything to make sure he wasn't damaged, even resorting to using a hairdryer to remove all traces of moisture.

She looked at me accusingly – clearly suspecting I'd tried to drown my rival in a jealous rage – but I swear it was the baby's doing.

I've even considered going to a marriage guidance counsellor but how do you admit to a complete stranger that your wife's in love with a computer toy boy?

It all came to a head the other day when I finally managed to win some of her attention and persuaded her to come upstairs for a 'cuddle'.

(Intimate moments are hard to come by when you've got four children, but the baby was asleep and the others were watching a video, so it was the perfect opportunity. After all, I'm still a game boy myself, given half a chance.)

Sadly, it wasn't to be. The baby started crying before we'd reached the top of the stairs and the moment was lost.

I grabbed him from his cot, brought him in to our bedroom and there she was, the brazen hussy, on the bed – with him!

"I'm just going to have a little play," she said casually.

Determined to revive our romance, I've secretly booked a night of luxury in a country hotel for our tenth anniversary.

I'd like to get her a really special present to mark the occasion. Ten years is a 'tin' wedding. I thought a new tin-opener might be nice.

Sadly, she has her own ideas. "If you're thinking of getting me an anniversary present, I'd really like my own Game Boy. A red one, preferably," she said.

It's over.

Things they don't say...

"IT *is* fair – I completely accept that."

Short cut to a rollicking

US dads have many burdens to carry through the assault course known as parenthood.

And they are symbolised by one supposedly useful invention – the baby carrier, the back-pack, the papoose, call it what you will.

After four children in seven years, I've reached the point where I feel naked without the latest little one sitting contentedly in the contraption on my back.

Life isn't the same without me staggering through life like a modern-day Quasimodo, with warm baby saliva dribbling in little rivulets down my neck.

It gets worse when, every now and again, the baby thinks it's a great game to spit his dummy on to the floor so I have to bend down to pick it up.

Halfway down, you start to lose your balance and getting back up isn't easy.

In fact, it's the fatherly equivalent of a pregnant elephant slithering back to her feet after slipping down a mudbank.

On walks down by the river, on marathon treks round the supermarket, it's always there, weighing me down.

Oh yes, the back-pack was a truly great invention.

And yet in all my years as a dad, I've never reached the point where I've kicked the back-pack. Until last weekend.

My wife, bless her, was in need of a rest after a week on her own with four kids.

I'd been away and she hadn't been at all well so I sent her to bed on Saturday afternoon for a lie down.

To enhance my bid to be the perfect husband and father, I decided to surprise her by cutting our (very big) lawn while she was asleep.

The three older children were happily plonked in front of a video with a bowl of crisps each, but the baby was never likely to let me get on with the job in hand.

So what did I do? I put him in the back-pack.

There I was, up and down the garden for a couple of hours, like a cart horse with an overweight jockey on his back, spraying sweat around like a water sprinkler, picking up discarded dummies every five minutes and generally making the garden look lovely.

By the time she came downstairs, I was recovering in an armchair with a beer can in my hand.

"What do you think of the lawn then?" I gasped.

"What setting did you have the mower on?" she replied.

"What do you mean?" I asked.

"You've cut it too short, haven't you? You're not supposed to cut grass that short on the first cut of the year. It kills it."

So basically, I was being told off for letting her have a rest, looking after four kids for the afternoon – and cutting the grass too well.

Like I said, us dads have many burdens to carry through our lives...

The things they say (about death)...

TWO little boys called Christopher and Alexander, from Hartlepool, were pondering the subject of death:
"See that bright star up there," said Alexander. "That's where my pet rabbit Fluffy is."
"That's nothing," replied Christopher. "My grandma's dog Candy went on the dustbin wagon."

GRANDMA Cicely Hall, of Darlington, was telling me how her youngest grandson Gareth was intrigued by her age.
"You're quite old aren't you Grannie," he said. "You could die soon, couldn't you?"
"Well, I suppose I could," she replied.
"Well tell me this," the boy went on, "when you get to heaven will God make you go on being an old woman or start you off again as a new baby?"

ENA Eastaugh, from Silksworth, Sunderland, keeps a photograph of her late husband in her purse. Alongside the picture is a list of telephone numbers of family and friends.
When Ena's five-year-old great grand-daughter Lauren Clements saw inside the purse, she asked: "Do you phone God to talk to Grandad Fred?"

SALLY Nixon, of North Cowton, was about four when she was discussing her grandad's death with her mum. After a pause, she said: "Do you know Mummy, God must have been really lonely before anyone died."

OVERHEARD by her grandma, Emma, aged six, asked her brother Josh, eight, a serious question: "Will you miss me when I die?"
"Not as much as Mum and Dad," replied Josh.
"Why's that? asked Emma.
"Because I've known them longer," came the reply.

ABI'S grandad had died and she was naturally very upset.
"I know how you can get up to heaven to see your Grandad," said her friend Rosie. "You have to put on your very best clothes and get on a bouncy castle and bounce high enough to see him."

JESSICA, seven, and her brother Robert, five, were talking about heaven.
"You know how Princess Diana went to heaven, don't you?" asked Jessica. "In a taxi with lots of flowers round her."

A FIVE-year-old, who must remain nameless, on the death of his grandad: "They'll be so pleased to see him in heaven that there'll be a big party and they'll be crashing cymbals together – that's what thunder is."

And getting old...

PHILIPPA Hudson, of Blackwell, Darlington, loves her chats with her dad at bedtime...
Dad: "What shall we talk about tonight?"
Philippa, aged eight, after a thoughtful pause: "Tell me about pensions."

ABI, who's only six, and has now left the North-East to live in Poland was sitting with her grandma and auntie and giving them both a long, hard look.
"What's the matter?" asked her Grandma.
"I was just wondering which of you has the most crumples," replied Abi.

Boys will be boys

ONE thing is guaranteed with little boys – they fight like Tom and Jerry. There's just something in their metabolism that makes them want to argue, wrestle or sword fight until they drop.

If I had a pound for all the times I've heard those immortal words "I had it first...No, you didn't, I had it first..." I'd be richer than any Lottery winner.

My big brother and I used to fight all the time. And now, a generation later, my boys are at it too.

I got so sick of our seven-year-old and his four-year-old brother fighting over anything and everything that I decided to get them out of the house for a while.

"Let's go for a nature ramble down to the river," I suggested, thinking it was a good, healthy pastime which would stop them knocking spots off each other.

In an attempt to make it more educational, I thought it would be a good idea to give them a pencil and a pad so they could make a note of all the different creatures we saw along the way.

The eagle-eyed seven-year-old spotted a blackbird in a tree – it went in his book.

He saw a crow on a rooftop – it went in his book.

He noticed a robin sitting on a fence – it went in his book.

He came across a rabbit – it went in his book (even though it had been squashed by a car).

"What about those insects crawling around inside the rabbit Dad, shall I put them down?" he asked.

"No, forget about them," I replied, trying not to think about them too hard.

His little brother was clearly feeling left out: "Look what I've found, Dad," he shouted excitedly, running ahead and pointing at the ground.

I couldn't see what he was talking about but he soon enlightened me: "It's a worm hole, Dad."

His big brother was quick to butt in: "You can't put a worm hole down – that's not a creature, it's a hole."

"Yes, you can," insisted his little rival.

"Can't," retorted his brother stubbornly.

"Can."

"Can't."

"Can."

"Can't."

Before I could get a word in edgewise, our peaceful nature ramble had descended into a fight.

I decided I'd had enough. When we got home, I took the seven-year-old into his bedroom for a "man to man talk".

"Look Christopher, you have to be nicer to Jack because he's a lot younger than you and you have to be more patient," I said in my sternest voice.

"But he just gets on my nerves, Dad," he insisted.

There was clearly a need to hammer home the message so I told him to think about all the things he liked about his little brother and all the things he'd miss if he wasn't around.

"I want you to stay in your room and write them all down on a piece of paper," I instructed.

Fifteen minutes later, I went back to his room to see if he'd completed the task: "Have you finished?" I asked.

"Yes Dad," he replied. "I've written down all the things I like about Jack and all the things I'd miss if he wasn't here."

My heart rose – this was a real breakthrough. I took the piece of paper from him and read it eagerly.

It was filled from top to bottom with one word repeated in thick, black felt tip: **"NOTHING, NOTHING, NOTHING, NOTHING, NOTHING, NOTHING, NOTHING, NOTHING, NOTHING."**

World Cup woe

IT was the day of England's first game in the World Cup. Everyone on the planet was watching it. Except me. I had to work.

There was only one thing for it – ask my wife, who hates football with a passion, to tape it for me and hope I could avoid the result.

Ear-plugs in place, all human contact avoided, car radio switched off, I managed to remain in blissful ignorance until I got home.

"Hi Dad," said my seven-year-old, who has no interest in football, "Engerla-a-a-and."

He had his arms raised jubilantly over his head. Of all the thousands of people I feared might spill the beans, it never dawned on me that it might be him. Him who wouldn't know a Seaman from a Seahorse. Him who wouldn't know Tony Adams from Morticia Adams.

"Two-nil, two-nil." Oh well, I hadn't really expected to get that far. And, anyway, the result made up for the disappointment. Once the kids were packed off to bed, I settled down with a can of beer to watch the victory unfold but couldn't find it on the tape.

"What tape's it on?" I asked.

"The one in the machine," my wife replied. It wasn't. I fast-forwarded, I rewound. I did it three times. She'd taped Channel 4 by mistake. Instead of England versus Tunisia, I had the chance to watch a women's chat show called Light Lunch. I could have thrown mine up.

"Oh well, you knew the result," she said.

If I'd taped the wrong channel when ER and that George Clooney fella were on, I'd have been vasectomied all over again. But this was only a football match. I could have cried. You see, football is a fantasy for us dads.

When the World Cup's on, you see them everywhere you look: sweaty, talentless dads, blinded by their dreams, playing footie with their kids wherever there's a blade of grass. When you're a dad, you can dribble the ball in and out of your little one's legs, blast it between a couple of jumpers and believe you're Alan Shearer scoring the World Cup-winning goal.

Take the couple of Geordie lads I watched playing footie with their kids at a picnic area. Both were wearing England shirts straining under the pressure of bulges Jimmy Five Bellies would have been proud of.

I had visions of the stitching giving way and the picnic area being flooded with Brown Ale and families swimming for their lives.

But these Dads – Dave and Stu – were blind to their physical shortcomings. They bamboozled their little ones with their not-so-silky skills, left toddlers crying on their bottoms after being "nutmegged" and hugged each other whenever they put the ball past the little girl in goal. The worst bit was when Stu scored, pulled his shirt over his head Ravanelli-style, and his enormous gut spilled out as if he'd given birth to a Space Hopper.

Dave even gave a running commentary in the style of John Motson: "Batty wins the ball, plays it through to Anderson, great balance, lovely ball to Owen, look at the pace of the Wonder Kid, Shearer's there – **GOOOOOOOOOAL!**"

Had Motto really been commentating, it would have been more like: "One Fat Dad steals the ball from a four-year-old, kicks it roughly in the direction of another Fat Dad, he wobbles along with the pace of a pregnant warthog, passes back to the other Fat Dad, who scuffs it past a five-year-old girl."

The only time the kids got a kick was when Dave and Stu took a beer break, cracking open a can of Broon each and having a good guzzle before jogging back to the field of play.

Gazza would have been proud of their idea of a light lunch. But what would Glenn Hoddle say?

Through thick and 'tin'

THERE'S no pleasing women sometimes is there?

My wife and I are celebrating ten years of marriage – ten golden years which have produced four kids, as well as streaks of grey hair and eyes with trademark black rings of which Chi-Chi the panda would have been proud.

Given the fact that there were some people at our wedding who staked money on it not lasting ten weeks, it was a milestone worth celebrating.

Fifty years is golden. Twenty five is silver. Ten years, apparently, is tin – so I bought my wife a nice, new, shiny tin-opener.

The one we've got is a bit dodgy and as old as the marriage, so I thought it would be a really useful and appropriate present. But, for some reason, she didn't seem too impressed. In fact, she threw it at me.

Like I said, women aren't easy to please.

On reflection, I decided she was probably worth something extra. After all – like most women – she's the one who's given up the most for the kids.

In fact, there have been times when I've marvelled at her ability to cope on precious little sleep and never-ending demands for attention (and that's just from me!).

Put simply – and at the risk of being over-sentimental – she's played a blinder as both a wife and a mum and I wanted her to know it.

So, with four kids in tow, I called in at a posh country hotel and booked a surprise weekend in the bridal suite, complete with four-poster bed, champagne in the room, and candle-lit dinner.

Grandma (she's been a star too) agreed to have all four of them for the weekend so we could have some time to ourselves for the first time since our eldest was born eight years ago.

It was worth every penny...

- We swam in the hotel pool and played tennis before dinner.
- We were serenaded in the restaurant by the resident singer's rendition of the Lionel Ritchie classic "Endless Love".
- We sipped champagne in our room and talked without anyone asking for a drink or to have their bottoms wiped.
- We actually spent the night side by side without me being kicked out into the bottom bunk, top bunk or any other bed which happened to have been vacated by one of our restless offspring.
- We got up at our leisure, instead of being dragged down to watch Tellytubbies at some unearthly hour.
- We had breakfast served to us instead of having to force it down the mouths of a fussy foursome who can't decide if they want Frosties, Rice Krispies or toast.
- We strolled around the hotel gardens, hand in hand, without anyone sitting astride my shoulders or strapped to my back.

And it was then that she looked at me, with undying love in her eyes, and said: "Are you missing the kids?"

It wasn't quite what I was expecting, but I had to admit that I was.

"So am I," she replied. "Let's go home."

It had been great to get away from it all – restful, romantic, and revitalising. So how come we couldn't wait to get back to the chaos?

Here's to the next ten years. Anyone fancy a tin-opener going cheap?

Things they don't say...

"YES, I agree it was my fault and I really am very sorry."

The things they say (about Christmas)...

FIFTY years ago, a little boy called Tom, from Darlington, was telling his mum that he'd like a fort for Christmas.

"Not a finking fort, a fighting fort," he added fortfully.

"SANTA, can you also remember to bring something for all the poor children in other countries who have to scrape up plants just to make some soup." – our eight-year-old to Santa on Christmas Eve.

"GRANDMA – did you know it's eight months today to Christmas Day?" – Nine-year-old Keith Anderson, from Washington, phoning his grandma on April 25.

"DAD – Mum told me to show you these and to tell you she hopes someone buys them for her for Christmas." – My little girl, handing me a Marks & Spencer carrier bag containing a pair of slippers.

OUR littlest one has been learning about the true meaning of Christmas at his nursery school.
"It's when Mary bought the baby cheeses," he explained.

UNCLE John was on the phone to the kids on Christmas Eve: "Have you been good all year?" he asked Jack, aged seven.
"I can't turn back history but I have brushed my teeth tonight, put my pyjamas on and tidied my bedroom for Santa coming," Jack replied.

HOW come Father Christmas brings us all these presents and you don't bring us any?" – Christopher Briggs, aged seven, of Nunthorpe, Middlesbrough, talking to his parents.

HELEN Sanderson, of Neasham, near Darlington, was eight when her dad bought her mum a new nightie for Christmas.
"It doesn't fit her," Helen announced to the family after her mum tried it on. "Mum's got to shrink."

JANET Paterson, from Dalton, near Darlington, recalls travelling on a bus to see Santa Claus and looking out of the window to see a small boy weeing up the wall.
"What's he doing?" she asked her Mum.
Her Mum, a little flustered, and not really knowing what to say, blurted out: "He's got a spout to wee up the wall with."
A little while later, Janet was sat on Santa's knee.
"What would you like for Christmas?" asked Santa.
"I'd like a little spout to wee up the wall with," answered Janet without hesitation.

P.S. THERE'S a fellow Dad in our office who shall be known only as Chris to save him from possible Mother's Union hit squads.
Guess what he got his wife for Christmas? AN IRON.
Amazingly, he's still walking around with all his faculties intact and still fails to see the problem: "It was a really nice one," he insisted when questioned.

Do I look stupid?

HOW come everyone seems to think us dads are stupid?

It is a question I came to ponder as I stood with our four children on Darlington railway station, saying goodbye to Mum, who was off to London for a school reunion.

"Goodbye Christopher, I love you. Goodbye Hannah, I love you. Goodbye Jack, I love you. Goodbye Max, I love you," she said to each of them in turn while giving them a hug and a kiss.

I got a kiss as well but the sentiment was somewhat different: "You won't forget to feed them will you?"

Let us just analyse this question for a moment: Would I be likely to starve my own children over the course of an entire weekend? Am I: a) stupid? b) cruel? c) suffering from acute amnesia?

Personally, I don't think any of them apply, so I couldn't help feeling insulted as the train snaked away and I considered the weekend ahead.

It wasn't so bad. OK, I had four children to cope with on my own, but it had its advantages.

By far the biggest was that I'd be able to watch the football without feeling guilty or having to be incredibly helpful for the two hours before kick-off.

Nevertheless, I couldn't get my wife's parting question out of my mind as we headed straight for McDonalds.

(Maybe it was my offended sub-conscious which instructed me to stuff the kids full of chicken nuggets and chips straight away in case I forgot for the next two days.)

"Bloomin' cheek," I thought to myself over a milkshake.

And yet my wife's not the only one who thinks I have the IQ to match a gnat's inside leg measurement. My Mum and Dad are exactly the same.

In fact, judging by some of the things they say, they obviously think I'm still at junior school. Things like:

- "Make sure that baby's well wrapped up." (Whenever he's had a cold in the freezing depths of winter.)
- "You won't let them play with any exposed electrical cables will you?"
- "Make sure they've got sun cream on." (When they're out in a heatwave.)
- "You won't let them go in the deep end on their own, will you?" (When we're at the swimming pool.)
- "Don't let them go too close to the lines, will you?" (When I mentioned that we were going to the railway station.)

I know they mean well, but – for the record – I'd like to point out the following:

1. I'm four years off being 40. (God, it was hard writing that bit.)
2. I have a responsible job.
3. I've successfully produced four healthy children.
4. I've voted in several General Elections.
5. I usually remember to wash behind my ears at least once a week.
6. I've been old enough to go into pubs on my own – and drink alcohol – for 18 years.

The weekend was bearable apart from a couple of hiccups: I forgot to get the washing in when it rained; the baby pulled his nappy off and made an unmentionable mess on the lounge carpet; and yes, the kids had to remind me that they hadn't had any tea – **BUT I WOULD HAVE GOT ROUND TO IT**.

Oh, I nearly forgot...

When I heard that a savage, man-eating tiger had escaped from the circus and was busy scoffing all the children in the village in the middle of a catastrophic earthquake, I told our kids it was OK to go out and play in the street.

That's all right isn't it?

Sick of family holidays

HOLIDAYS used to be relaxing. Lying on a beach, reading trashy novels and enjoying long, leisurely meals in the sun.

Not any more...

For months, I'd been looking forward to a long weekend away at Center Parcs in Sherwood Forest. A time to be with the family, take it easy, breathe fresh air, and play a bit of sport. I couldn't wait.

It started going downhill on the first night in our idyllic woodland cabin. We were just settling down to a bottle of wine when the sound that every parent dreads – the sound of a child being sick – emanated from a bedroom.

There'd been no time to grab a bowl. The contents of his stomach were everywhere and the vomiting was to continue for most of the night.

The trouble with sickness bugs in families is that you know, with a gloomy inevitability, that the domino effect will quickly take over. It is only a matter of time before the rest of the family goes down one by one.

Though shattered due to lack of sleep, we did our best to make the most of the break. We played crazy golf, hired bikes, I exhausted myself propelling a child-laden pedal boat across a large lake (why are pedalos built so you feel like you're pedalling through treacle?), we splashed around for hours in the pool, and I went for a horse ride, the after-effects of which brought back painful memories of my vasectomy.

Through it all, the sickness kept flowing faster than the wild water rapids in the leisure pool. The baby, followed by his sister, succumbed to the dreaded lurgy.

In a bid to escape the sick bay, I took our eldest – at that point still waiting to be struck down – for an evening swim. We cycled to the pool, left our bikes in the cycle park, and headed for the water.

Two hours later, we emerged into the darkness that had descended across the forest and went to collect the bikes.

There was a slight problem. The boy couldn't remember where he'd parked his. There were thousands of bikes locked up in the bike park and he didn't have a clue which was the right one.

"I think I parked it near a tree," he said, sheepishly, as my blood pressure soared higher than the pines.

WE WERE IN THE MIDDLE OF A FOREST FOR GOD'S SAKE. THERE WERE MORE TREES THAN BIKES!

And so began the great bike hunt. From 10pm to midnight, we tried the key in the lock of every bike that resembled his – over and over and over again. It was the biggest job since Prince Charming set out to find the foot to fit Cinderella's slipper.

Unlike the Prince, we never found the right fit. What happened to the bike remains a mystery. Sick as parrots, we trudged home to find the vomit still in full flow.

The bug finally hit me on the way home up the A1, just after the Doncaster turn-off. There was nothing else for it but to pull over into a lay-by, where I threw up violently behind a hedgerow. (Apologies to the splashed hedgehog.)

From there, the journey was completed in 20-minute bursts between lay-bys.

Sometimes, just sometimes, I get sick of being a dad...

A day to treasure

SO there I was, down by the river early on a Sunday morning, digging a dirty big hole with my garden spade.

You find yourself in all kinds of peculiar situations when you're a dad... situations which frequently require explanation.

"It's OK – I haven't robbed a bank," I found myself saying to a man walking his dog.

I couldn't help feeling like a criminal as I dug deeper and tried the large black box in the hole for size.

"It's for a treasure hunt," I explained to another dog-walker, who nodded silently.

As I finally shovelled the last spadeful of earth on top of the treasure chest, I was convinced that anyone watching would suspect I'd just buried a murdered body.

The truth was that our eldest had requested an Enid Blyton Adventure Party for his eighth birthday. I had to write a special Famous Five story and he'd invite friends to play the roles.

He would play Julian, of course. His best friend James would be Dick, and schoolfriends Rachel and Becky would be Anne and George respectively. Oh, and Timmy the mongrel would be played by a stuffed dog called Tuffy who lives on top of a bedroom wardrobe.

The invitations were sent, and the story – The Mystery of Rabbit Hill – was penned.

The plot, about evil poachers shooting rabbits and selling their fur for diamonds, culminated with clues pinned to trees and fences, leading the "Famous Five" to the treasure. I felt rather proud as I walked home with my muddy spade over my shoulder.

Julian was on tenterhooks as midday approached. Anne arrived first, closely followed by George.

"I say you two," he said, Julian-like. "Seems like a jolly good day for an adventure. Hurrah!" (He's a strange child at times.)

Timmy was waiting patiently in a rucksack, along with Julian's compass, a piece of string, pencil and paper, torch and elastic band.

But disaster was about to strike. The crucial fifth member of the Famous Five hadn't turned up. We rang his house but there was no answer. What on earth could have gone wrong?

"Oh, Dad, what am I going to do without a Dick?" cried Julian, exasperated.

It was a question I found hard to answer, but we urgently needed a substitute Dick and there wasn't much choice. It was either the birthday boy's six-year-old sister or four-year-old brother. There were drawbacks with both: his sister's a girl, and his little brother's considered a pain in the bum.

"Do you think you could be a Dick?" he asked his sister, reluctantly. She readily agreed and the party was back on.

The story was read and the first clue handed out. Gradually, the Famous Five followed the clues to the river and eventually discovered the dropped emerald which marked the place where they needed to dig.

Their faces when they finally hit something solid were a picture. And again when they opened the old treasure chest to find the diamonds – coloured glass beads – inside.

We finished off the adventure with a riverside picnic, complete with cream cakes and lashings of ginger beer.

"Urgh – that ginger beer's disgusting," squealed Dick, spitting it out and splashing 'his' flowery dress.

Well, nothing can be perfect. As to what happened to the real Dick, it remains a mystery...

Hunger takes the biscuit

OF all the things children say over and over again, "I'm starving" has got to be up there near the top of the list.

"Can I have a biscuit Dad?"

"No, you'll be having your tea soon."

"Aw, but Dad, I'm really, really starving."

Mum, who is much harder than me, decided she'd had enough of hearing the familiar cry every time they hadn't eaten for more than two minutes.

"You have no idea what starving means," she said to blank looks. "There are some children who don't get a thing to eat for days and days."

So, after tea one night, she boldly announced to our three older children that they were going to have a "no food day" to teach them what it was really like to be hungry.

"Fine," they replied with all the confidence inspired by newly-filled stomachs.

"We'll do it one day next week," suggested Mum.

"Oh, can we do it tomorrow?" replied seven-year-old Hannah, polishing off her third yoghurt for dessert.

The day of fasting dawned and five-year-old Jack was reminded that this was the day he would really find out what it was like to be starving. They could have breakfast but then just drinks for the rest of the day.

"Can I have fish and chips for breakfast with extra chips?" replied Jack in a sudden panic.

The answer was "no" but they all scoffed as many scotch pancakes as they could manage to fit in.

Like I said, my wife can be hard. When lunch-time arrived, she decided to go shopping to pile on the agony.

Biscuits, cakes, and crisps were piled into the trolley. Torture at its most agonising.

"You're just being mean," said Christopher, before adding: "Can we get some of those and some of those and some of those for tomorrow?"

Even the checkout assistant was told that they'd been "forced" into having a "no food day".

They arrived back at the house at 2pm. It was three-and-a-half hours since breakfast and Hannah announced that she was so weak she could "hardly walk".

"Can we have lunch now, I'm dying?" said Jack, pulling a pig of a face.

"No," said Mum. But, not being quite as hard as she likes to make out, she compromised by saying that they could have tea.

"Yes!" shouted Jack, punching the air and running to tell his big brother the wonderful news.

He was back two minutes later to ask: "Is it tea-time yet?"

He then decided he needed to set the kitchen timer for the exact amount of time left before he could eat.

Over the next two-and-a-half hours, he proceeded to wear a track between the lounge and the kitchen every two minutes to check the timer's progress.

Finally, it was tea-time: "This is the best tea we've ever had," Jack declared.

Mum was busy giving them a lecture about the poor and starving children in places like Africa, but everyone was far too busy eating to take much notice.

Things they don't say...

"I WON'T eat these sweets before my dinner. I'll save them for later."

Pudding on the agony

IT'S been another week for worrying in our house.

My dad started it. He phoned after seeing the news about a fishing boat's encounter with a great white shark off the coast of Italy.

"You'll have to watch those bairns," he said.

"Sorry?" I replied.

"It's that global warming. The sharks are coming further north," he explained.

"I doubt they'll get as far as Redcar," I reasoned.

"You never know," he insisted. He could worry for England, my dad.

To be honest, we had more pressing reasons to worry. Our third born – Jack – was starting school and you always worry about them, don't you?

Would he like his teacher? Would he be self-conscious about his new glasses? Would he wipe his bottom properly? Would he like school dinners?

It was the latter question which worried me most. I hated school dinners.

I still cringe when I remember being kept back in my early school days because I wouldn't eat carrots, or cabbage, or peas, or anything that wasn't a chip.

I hated the smell of school dinners, especially the stew which lingered like a sewage leak for days.

And the sight of that white stuff that looked like it had been mixed with frog spawn, always made me feel sick.

The only fond memories I have of school dinners were when I got to be a "server" in the last year of junior school.

I was able to give myself 90 per cent of the chips and let the little ones on my table starve.

But then I was found out and got lines – "I must not be greedy and give myself all the chips" – 100 times.

So, given the psychological scars, I was naturally fretting about how Jack would react.

I needn't have worried. He's taken to school dinners like a great white shark takes to eating small children bathing off Seaton Carew.

"How did it go?" I asked him after his first day.

"Great," he replied. Then his eyes lit up and he started running around as if he'd scored a goal in the Cup Final, shouting: **"WE HAD CHOCOLATE SPONGE!"**

"What did you do at school today, Jack?" I enquired the next day.

"Can't remember," he replied wearily.

"You must remember something," I persisted.

"Just the pudding."

"What was it?"

"Custard with a thing in the middle."

"What thing?"

"Dunno. Just a brown thing and I didn't like it so I just eated the custard – with a spoon." What else would he eat it with?

Anyway, from talking to other dads, it seems school dinners have been the dominant subject in lots of homes over the past few days.

One colleague told me how his little boy had been informed by his older brother not to worry about school dinners because the new-starters always went first and had the choice of everything.

The little lad, taking his brother's words literally, went up to the serving counter and demanded everything he could see.

"I'll have that and that and some of that and a few of those and a bit of that and, and, and."

"You can't have sausages and pie," explained the dinner lady patiently. "It's one or the other."

"No, I can have everything," the boy insisted. "Me brother told me."

God help the other kids if he ever gets to be a server...

Who ya gonna call? Fast cabs!

I NEVER wanted to be a taxi driver... When I was little, I dreamed of being a World Cup-winning footballer, or a Wimbledon-winning tennis player.

If those dreams didn't come true, my back-up ambition was to be a quantity surveyor. (I had no idea what one did but it sounded impressive.) My dad, a steelworker all his life, wanted me to be a welder.

In the end, I settled on being a journalist on the grounds that – coming from a home that always had the Daily Mirror – I figured that it couldn't be too difficult.

But the notion of being a taxi driver never once crossed my mind – until I became a dad. Now, the journalism is squeezed in between operating a taxi service for the kids: "FAST CABS" I call it. FAST stands for "Father's A Soft Touch".

It's unbelievable. Saturday mornings are the worst. Our eldest has to be dropped off at his drama class, his sister has to be delivered to gymnastics lessons, and their little brother has to get to soft play – all within 20 minutes of each other at different venues around the town.

Monday night is taekwondo night. That's when our eight-year-old learns self-defence techniques which he tests out on the taxi driver back home, leaving him with painful memories of his not-so-distant vasectomy when a kick intended to take his legs away goes about a foot too high.

Tuesday night is Rainbows night for our little girl. Rainbows is one step down from Brownies and a lot gentler than taekwondo, but it still requires a taxi ride.

Crammed in between are the endless list of parties they have to be taken to and collected from. I've lost count of the number of times the FAST CABS hotline has rung at work with the message: "Christopher/Hannah/Jack's at a party tonight. They need picking up at 7pm."

I've started answering like a cabbie: "Wilco – over and out, grumble, grumble."

I've even bought myself an A-Z street-planner in case I get lost en route.

And this week, there was yet another addition to the hackney carriage headache. The eldest joined a chess club which meets on Friday evenings.

Friday evenings used to mark the end of a hard week in the day job. They were for relaxing with a glass of red wine in front of the telly.

Not anymore. It's off to the chess club for 8pm to sit around for an hour while the boy embarks on becoming the new Kasparov.

And do you know what he had the cheek to say after his first night on the boards? "You can wait in the car next week if you like, Dad."

I'm nothing more than a pawn in his little game, and it's certain to carry on for years to come.

"Wait 'til they're teenagers and you're sitting at the wheel outside a nightclub waiting for your daughter to stop canoodling with her new boyfriend," a more mature dad said to me the other day. I nearly crash the car whenever I think of it.

But let me tell you this: it may be a long road ahead, but the meter's running – and one day, it'll be pay-back time!

Old and out of focus

IT'S hard getting old. At 36, I'm starting to feel ancient and it's got a lot to do with the kids.

"Dad, you're really, really old aren't you?" said my five-year-old son, Jack, the other day. "You're so old your bones are all creaky aren't they?"

Oh, I've been going grey at the edges for a while – is it any wonder? – and I think I'm losing my hair, but I'm in denial.

But there's no escape: "Dad, when you're fully bald can I polish your head with a soft cloth?" the same five-year-old asked not so long back. I refused to answer.

Lots of other little things make you feel that life's racing by. Our eldest, for example, has reached the age where he won't kiss either me or his mum in public.

His mum insists on a kiss in the car, away from prying eyes, but I only get a kiss these days if we're locked safely in the house.

"Don't I get a hug?" I shouted after him when I dropped him off at school last week.

"Oh boy," was his disgusted response before turning to his friend, muttering "Fathers" under his breath, and stomping off.

But what really, really, really made me feel old was a trip to the opticians. For months, my contact lenses have been giving me trouble. I've been viewing life through a mist and I knew something was wrong.

The examination was long and thorough before the optician's verdict was delivered: "You've got a dry eye problem," he declared.

"A dry eye problem – what causes that?" I asked.

"It's just your age – you're drying out," he explained matter-of-factly.

"Drying out?"

"Yes, your body dries out the older you get."

I glanced at myself in the mirror at the other end of the room and saw a shrivelled prune looking back at me.

The kindly optician went on to explain that every time you blink it brings a tear down to keep the eye moist.

"Your tears are poor quality – they're drying out very quickly."

Poor quality tears? My God, this was serious.

"You need to keep your eyes moist. You could try blinking more often – and do you find that your eyes water when you yawn?"

"Hang on a bit," I thought to myself. "I can't go through life as a blinking, yawning idiot – I'd get locked up."

In the end, there was nothing else for it. I had to give in to the idea of wearing glasses for the rest of my life.

After trying on at least 4,000 pairs, I chose what I considered to be quite a modern style.

I modelled them for the kids and wished I hadn't. Jack looked, pondered and shouted: "Cool – you look like a Grandad!"

The things they say...

IT is sheer coincidence that this same five-year-old was lying on my lap the other night, gazing up at me with loving fascination in his eyes and a smile on his face.

There was a cartoon on the box but it didn't matter. He had his back turned to the screen as he gazed up admiringly at his good old dad.

His mum noticed and smiled contentedly at the bonding taking place between father and son.

"Ahh, do you love me?" I asked him quietly.

"No Dad, I'm just watching the telly through the reflection in your glasses," came the reply.

The things they say...

A LITTLE five-year-old lad called Luke McArthur, from Guisborough, was all dressed up in his new outfit for Easter and being admired by his grandma.

"Ooh, you look lovely," she cooed. "Where did you get your new shirt and tie from?"

"Me mam got me them from Marks and Expensive," he replied, proudly.

"MY mam and dad have just had a baby boy called Connor, so now I'm a big brother. I love my brother more than all the sweets in the world. I have asked my mam to bring me a sister next time." – Reece Clark, aged 4, of Hartlepool.

MUM Julie Bowes, of Bishop Auckland: "I just can't remember the name – it's on the tip of my tongue."

Daughter Aysha: "Well, stick it out and I'll tell you."

"DAD, when I grow up, will I have a really big nose like you?" – Our Jack, aged four.

MATTHEW Jones, one of three boys in a Darlington family, was six years old when he turned to his mum and said: "Mum, why are we all boys?"

His mum, not sure what to say, replied that it was just the way God had made them.

Matthew wasn't satisfied: "I know why it is – it's because of the way we comb our hair."

MATTHEW was also responsible for coming home from school one day and saying: "Mum, there's a word we mustn't say."

"What is it?" asked his mum.

"I can't tell you – I mustn't say it," said Matthew.

"You can tell me – I'm your mum," she replied, fearing the worst.

Reluctantly, Matthew told her what it was: "We mustn't say the word 'cos'".

"Cos?" asked his mum.

"Yes," said Matthew. "The teacher says we have to say 'because.'"

"IMAGINE how many pots of paint you'd need to paint Mummy's big bottom." – Our Christopher while the house was being decorated.

"AW – why can't we have a babysitter?" – My beloved daughter after I broke the news to her and her brothers that mum was going out for the night and I was going to be looking after them.

"DAD, quick, the telly's run out of petrol." – Our four-year-old when the TV conked out in the middle of his favourite cartoon.

Another string to his bow

YOU may recall how we nearly poisoned next door's cat.

The poor, unsuspecting puss was sick to its boots after scoffing the week-old, rancid remains of our pet goldfish which the kids had left in a match-box coffin on the garden table prior to its forgotten burial.

Well, the agonised wailing of that food-poisoned feline was possibly the worst sound I've ever heard – until the boy got a cello.

All kids seem to go through a "I want to learn a musical instrument" period.

When I was at school, I made do with a recorder and I can still play 'The Grand Old Duke of York' on request.

But a cello? The last thing you need when you've got four kids is an oversized violin that takes up as much space as a well-fed teenager.

"Why did you choose a cello?" I enquired when the boy came home from school with his new-found pride and joy.

"Well, I asked for a trumpet but they'd all gone, and I asked for a trombone and they'd all gone, and I asked for one of those 'ufunnyum' things but they'd all gone, so I got a cello."

"What was wrong with a nice little recorder?" I asked.

"Recorders are boring, Dad," he protested.

"I can play 'The Grand Old Duke of York' on one," I went on, enthusiastically.

"I know, Dad, but please don't," he said.

So a cello it is – all because he was at the end of the queue when the other (smaller) instruments were handed out.

Now we have to sit and listen to him play – and Julian Lloyd-Webber he ain't.

"Do you want to hear my tune, Dad?" he asked the other day.

With his giant instrument between his legs, and a serious look on his face, he proceeded to produce a noise whch sounded like a posse of alley cats which had just eaten a lorry-load of dead fish injected with paraquat, let alone one miserable moggy with a rotten goldfish inside him.

"It's a tune I made up. It hasn't got a name yet," he explained.

"How about 'Requiem For A Tortured Tomcat'?" I suggested.

"That's a stupid name," he replied, matter-of-factly.

We even have to pay for the privilege of this latest episode in our lives – £17 a term to hire and insure the cello under a school music scheme.

I bet a recorder would only have cost a couple of quid.

Still, I suppose it could have been worse. I've got a friend whose little boy has asked for a set of drums for Christmas. The dad's asked Santa for some ear plugs.

And, who knows, the boy might prove us wrong and end up with another string to his bow.

We could even be in demand as a duo – him on the cello, me on the recorder.

All together now: "Oh, The Grand Old Duke of York, he had ten thousand men..."

Things they don't say...

"I'M REALLY pleased we've got some maths homework tonight – I'll get it done straight away."

Waking up with Big Bum & co.

TAKE a look at this list, carefully compiled in alphabetical order to guard against accusations of favouritism...

Babsy the lamb, Baggy the rabbit, Beany the cow, Big Bum the hippo, Big Tooth the walrus, Bouncer the rabbit, Chicken Pox the chicken, Christopher the cat, Curly 'C' the rabbit, Fluff the rabbit, Ginger the teddy, Hattie the bear, Iggy the iguana, Jess the cat, Longneck the giraffe, Michelle the turtle, Milk the cow, Peter the dog, Plop the owl, Pyjamas the teddy, Snowflake the lamb, Spotty the dog, Squeak the rat, Stripey the zebra, Sugar the horse, Teddy the bear, Tigger the tiger, Tuffy the dog, Whitey the cat, Winnie the Pooh, and yet another bear called Yoghurt.

They are all the cuddly toys that live in our house, taking it in turns to sleep with our four children. I have no doubt I could have named more but I got bored counting.

In short, we have more cuddly toys than we know what to with... more than Toys R Us could flog in an average Christmas...more than enough to fill The Generation Game's conveyor belt for decades to come.

It can be embarrassing. Many has been the time I've been kicked out of the marital bed by one of the kids and forced to share a top bunk or bottom bunk with Chicken Pox, Milk, Yoghurt, Sugar, Longneck, Ginger, Hattie or any combination of the others.

And many has been the time I've woken into semi-consciousness, not knowing which bed I'm in, and in the half-light struggled to identify my sleeping partner: Big Bum the Hippo or beloved wife?

At least once, amid the confusion, I've whispered "Do you fancy a morning cuddle?"

to Beany the cow. I'm sure I once asked Plop the owl if she wanted a cup of tea bringing up, and I've definitely told Big Tooth to stop snoring.

We've had to have many secret clear-outs to keep down the numbers, and the children's wards of local hospitals have been well stocked by our cuddly cast-offs over the years.

I remember once having to smuggle Timmy, the giant stuffed St Bernard, out of the house inside a black bin bag. As I shoved him into the car boot under the cover of darkness, I couldn't help feeling like a Brookside murderer, preparing to dispose of a body.

But there are some favoured cuddly toys that will never be dumped – like Iggy the Iguana for instance.

Jack, our five-year-old, doesn't go anywhere unless Iggy's with him. He had to go into hospital a few weeks ago for an operation to remove a piece of glass which had become embedded in his foot.

It's always a worrying time when one of your children has to have general anaesthetic, but I couldn't help laughing out loud when I called at the hospital to see Jack after his operation.

There he was, lying on his bed with his foot swathed in a whopping great bandage. And there next to him was Iggy, also with his foot wrapped in a thick dressing. The nurses had thoughtfully bandaged Iggy's foot to make Jack feel better.

"How are you feeling?" I asked.

"It hurts a lot Dad," he replied.

"Aw, and has Iggy had to have an operation too?" I enquired, sympathetically.

"Don't be stupid Dad – he's just a cuddly toy," came the reply.

I'm no smuggler

JUST when you think they're growing up, something happens to remind you that they're not...

Last time round, this column was reflecting on how an army of cuddly toys had gradually taken over the house – Winnie the Pooh, Iggy the iguana, Big Bum the hippo, Babsy the lamb, Plop the owl and Longneck the giraffe to name just a few.

A large number of them had travelled to work with me so they could have their photograph taken for the paper.

Very well behaved they were too – but little did I know that a tearful drama was about to unfold.

The evening after the photo-shoot, the stuffed animals were unceremoniously shoved back into a bin bag, and thrown onto the back seat of the car for the journey home.

On the way, I was under instruction to pick up our eldest from his weekly taekwondo class at the local community centre.

The boy seemed fine when I collected him, but he became strangely subdued when he climbed into the car.

"How was taekwondo?" I asked.

"Fine," he replied, morosely.

He appeared to be crying. "Are you OK?" I enquired.

"Yes – I've just got something in my eye."

"Are you sure? Has anyone been bullying you or anything?"

"No."

While he would be normally full of chat, the journey was completed in silence. When we arrived home, he went straight upstairs for a bath.

"I think there's something wrong with Christopher," I told his mum. "I'm worried he might have been picked on or something."

She went upstairs to try to get to the bottom of it: "What's wrong? Has something upset you?" she asked.

"I can't bring myself to talk about it," he said, bursting into tears.

Eventually, she coaxed it out of him: "It's just that Dad's been trying to smuggle the cuddly toys out of the house so he can give them away to a Christmas fair," he sobbed.

"I spotted them all in a bin bag in the back of his car.

"I know I'm eight now and I shouldn't be upset about things like this but I can't bear the thought of never sleeping with them again. I want them until I'm at least 14."

It was a full hour before we managed to convince him of the truth: "You're lying, I know you are. You're trying to get rid of them," he kept saying.

"I wouldn't do that to you," I promised (though I have to admit that it's crossed my mind once or twice).

When he fell asleep that night, Winnie, Big Bum, and co. were being cuddled more tightly than ever.

After all, there's no rush to grow up is there?

Things they don't say...

DAD, you're a really good dancer – you don't embarrass me one bit. All my friends think you're dead cool."

The things they say

A LITTLE boy called Patrick, aged five, had fallen over in the playground at his North Yorkshire school and was bleeding from the mouth so badly that his mum decided to take him to the doctor's.

Every time he opened his mouth, the blood flowed, so his mum told him not to talk. He kept quiet all the way until he could resist it no longer: "Mum, am I allowed to cry?" he asked.

OUR Jack: "Mum, can I ask you about a swear word?"
Mum: "Go on then."
Jack: "Can children say 'bloomin?'"
Mum: "I suppose so – they say it in Mary Poppins."
Jack: "Right – I'm going to say it then."
Mum: "OK."
Jack: "You're a bloody, bloomin', buggery thing."

LOUISE Holland, a member of Carlton WI, remembers her grandad having a thick, prickly moustache.
And when she was a little girl she asked a question which tickled everyone:
"Did grandma hit grandad with a scrubbing brush?"

"DAD, dad, I think I've got a PUBLIC hair!" A friend's six-year-old, running downstairs with his pyjama trousers round his ankles.

"MUM, is diarrhoea a cousin of flu?" – our six-year-old Jack after being told that germs are often related.

ONE young girl, who must remain nameless to save her parents' embarrassment, was visiting a house which had pretty mobiles in the nursery. "Do you have mobiles on the ceiling in your house?" she was asked. "No," she replied. "Just lots of cobwebs."

"DADDY, I'll love you even when you're bald and fat and wearing someone else's teeth." – my little girl, aged seven.

"GRANDAD, if you keep wearing those vests at night, your boobies will never grow properly." – Kate, aged nine, as told by her grandma at a Women's Institute meeting in Belmont, Durham.

THANKS to Karen Bowlzer, of Shadforth WI, Durham, for this story about her husband Steve . . .
When Steve was eight, he had a white teddy bear called Snowy (sorry Steve but your secret's out now). His younger sister Sue had a cuddly toy rabbit and they were arguing about which one was the whitest.
"My teddy's whiter than your rabbit," taunted Steve.
"Not any more it's not," replied Sue as she grabbed Snowy and shoved him up the chimney.

Last among equals...

IT'S been a long time coming, but the boy has finally found football.

The moment I'd dreamed of came a few weeks ago when he said: "Dad, could we go to a real football match sometime?"

He's eight now and I was beginning to think he'd never share my passion for the beautiful game. So it was with stomach-churning excitement that we headed to the Riverside for Middlesbrough versus Nottingham Forest in the Premiership.

His face beamed like a light being switched on when he climbed the steps and saw the shining jewel of the emerald green pitch.

And he cheered with everyone else when they announced the name of the prodigal son, Gazza, returning after his spell in a alcohol addiction clinic.

"This is what being a dad is all about," I thought to myself as I watched the ever-changing emotions on the boy's face.

But it soon became clear that he has a long way to go before he gets in the swing of things. When a Middlesbrough goal was disallowed, the tribal crowd bayed for the referee's blood: "You blind ******* referee... you useless ******* ****... get yer ******* eyes tested." You know the kind of thing.

The boy, still blessed with innocence, simply sighed and said: "I think I'll have to give that referee a piece of my mind."

I had hoped that the occasion would awaken ambitions for him to become a great striker, a midfield genius, a majestic defender, or a cat-like goalie.

It didn't quite work out like that. At full-time, he declared that he wants to be a referee.

It was bound to end in tears. He came home a few nights later to announce that he'd had a bit of trouble at school.

His class had been playing footie and he'd sent Jack Dell off for two bookable offences (he'd even gone to the lengths of having red and yellow cards made).

"The trouble was that it was Jack's ball so he went off with it, and all the others started picking on me because I'd sent him off," he explained. "I'm not sure I want to be a ref anymore."

But setback number one was nothing compared to setback number two, which may go down in history as a bigger psychological blow than the mental torture inflicted on Paul Gascoigne by his sensational omission from Glenn Hoddle's World Cup squad.

The boy came home the other day and I asked if he'd played football at lunchtime.

"Don't want to talk about it," he replied, morosely.

"Why, what happened?"

"They were picking the teams and there was only two of us left and I was the last one to get picked – and it was so embarrassing," he blurted out, tears welling up in his eyes.

It's a defining moment in any little boy's life and I remember it well.

If you're the first to be picked, you become a cult figure.

In the first six, and you're looked up to.

If you're among the dregs, you might as well walk round in a T-shirt proclaiming: "I'm inadequate."

And if you're the last of all, it's just too horrible to contemplate.

"Maybe you'll get picked first next time," I counselled.

"No I won't. I'm the worst player in the school," he sobbed.

"That's not true."

"Yes it is. **THEY EVEN PICKED RACHEL ALBAN BEFORE ME!**"

"Oh," I said, struggling to find the words.

He hasn't booked in to a rehabilitation clinic just yet, but it's probably only a matter of time.

Driving me up the wall

LIFE'S just one long lesson – and history is the subject of the moment.

Take the Romans. Please take the Romans, because they're driving me up the wall – Hadrian's to be exact.

The boy has been learning all about the Romans and he's become obsessed. He's gone from thinking I grew up in Victorian times to believing I was the son of a centurion instead of an electrician's mate down Lackenby steelworks.

Tired of being asked endless questions about Roman life, I gave in to his repeated requests to visit Hadrian's Wall in Northumberland.

"Can we go, Dad, can we, Dad, can we? It was built to keep the Scots out you know, Dad, and a fierce tribe called the Pixies. They wanted to fight the Kilts but they weren't very good fighters so they paid the Angelo Saxons to do their fighting for them," he explained, excitedly.

It took us so long to drive to a place called Housesteads, in the middle of nowhere, on a dark, freezing December day that daylight was fading fast by the time we arrived.

If I've visited a bleaker place I've forgotten it. Quite why the Pixies wanted to capture it, and why the Angelo Saxons and the Kilts wanted to stop them, heaven only knows.

"Wow, look at that bloomin' wall – amazing," the boy exclaimed. Then he lost interest within seconds and shouted: "Let's go see the fort."

Forts are generally more exciting than walls. But he was only interested in finding one thing – the Roman toilets. Why is it that boys are fascinated by anything to do with toilets?

"The toilets must be round here somewhere, Dad," he kept saying as the darkness crept up.

And then he suddenly shrieked and pointed to a circle of bricks: "Dad, quick, here's the toilet. Look – that's where they did their whatsits!"

An American family wandering nearby looked bemused as the boy expounded loudly on his remarkable knowledge of Roman loos.

"Guess what, Dad, they used to either have their own piece of moss to wipe their bums with or they could have a sponge on the end of a stick to share with a few others."

Doesn't it make you glad you're not a Roman? Anyway, the Romans weren't half as much bother as last term's history subject, the Ancient Greeks.

The boy came home every night with tales of the Minotaur, Zeus, Hercules and Medusa – "she could turn you to stone with just one look," he explained. (I glanced at his mum but said nothing.)

It all came to an exciting climax when his teacher, Mr Coates, decided it would help the past come to life if the boy's class tasted some authentic Greek grub.

Pitta bread, hummus, olives and figs were all laid out for the children to try. The boy, a picky eater at the best of times, didn't fancy any of it.

"I don't like it," he kept saying.

"Just try some," Mr Coates kept urging.

The boy tried a bit of pitta, tasted a little hummus, and then licked an olive, pulling the kind of face you pull if you're ordered to swallow arsenic.

It was the figs that really made him blanch: "I can't eat them," he insisted.

"You might like them," the teacher persisted.

The boy eventually ate one – and promptly vomited all over Mr Coates' piano stool.

Oh yes, life's just one long lesson…

Christmas? It flu by

IF I'd known what Santa was going to bring me for Christmas, I'd have told him to stuff it.

Flu – merciless, miserable, bone-aching, energy-sapping, appetite-shrinking – flu. That's what I got for Christmas. And Santa made sure I really suffered.

I knew it was coming. One by one, the kids and their Mum had been struck down by the ghastly virus in the run-up to the big day. And with perfect timing, sod's law decreed that I should start to go downhill on Christmas Eve.

I did my best to be jolly when Santa (sounding suspiciously like a family friend) made his usual magical visit to the house. I think I might have even forced a smile when I noticed what the kids had left him on the mantelpiece: Some hot chocolate, a mince pie, two Rich Tea biscuits and a Fox's Glacier Mint which had been unwrapped and then wrapped again.

"Ho, ho, ho, merry Christmas," he bellowed as he stepped into the kids' bedrooms.

"What would you like me to bring you tonight?" he asked our eldest, who has grown into a cocky but not-quite-ready-to-disbelieve eight-year-old.

The boy reeled off his list before adding: "Oh, and can you bring my dad a wig because this is his last year with any hair." Very funny.

Never mind new hair, it was a new head I needed by the time Christmas morning arrived. The one I had felt like it had been run over by a herd of stampeding reindeer.

It is a well-known medical fact that men feel pain more acutely than women. They must because when my wife had flu, she managed to look after four children AND finish all the Christmas preparations.

But men get it so bad that they can hardly move. They need rest. They need constant attention. They need to be listened to when they groan. And, most of all, they need peace and quiet.

On that last point, Christmas is the worst possible time to get flu. And it's all Santa's fault.

In the old man's infinite wisdom, he brought our baby something called 'The Dalmatian Chase'. This involves a litter of puppies being lifted one by one to the top of a staircase so they can slide down a roller-coaster. They keep going round and round and the baby loves it.

The trouble is that the puppies bark all the time – an incessant, thoroughly irritating, high-pitched yap. Over and over and over and over and over and over again. They don't stop barking.

You can move to different rooms, you can pile dozens of pillows over your head, but you can still hear them: "Yelp, yelp, yelp, yelp, yelp, yelp, yelp, yelp, yelp."

It would be enough to drive a healthy man mad, but for someone battling the temptation to walk through death's door and declare "Take me, take me, just stop it hurting," it was all too much.

By Boxing Day night, I had hallucinatory thoughts of knocking the spots off the little dalmatians with a bloomin' big hammer from a toolbox of a Christmas past.

And when it wasn't the puppies, it was Buzz Lightyear repeating "To infinity and beyond" or Woody shouting "Reach for the sky" or a fire engine's siren going off, or computer games playing sickeningly-catchy robotic tunes, or the Dyson junior vacuum cleaner making more of a racket than the adult version, or crackers going bang, or party poppers going pop, or kids shouting "Gerrof! Who said you could play with that?"

More had been spent on presents in our house than the average Geoffrey Robinson loan – and every single one of them made horribly loud noises.

Santa, I love you like a brother. But give me another Christmas like that, and I'll break your legs.

Man or a mouse?

DADS get the blame for everything. It's an undeniable fact.

We get blamed for the weather, as in: "I told you we should have brought their coats."

We get blamed when they're naughty, as in: "They get that from you."

We get blamed for not taking them out to play football enough... then we get blamed when they come back caked in mud.

We get blamed for wasting money on cards and gifts on Mother's Day... and we get blamed when we forget.

I'm regularly blamed for hair-dos that go wrong, the children being late for school, the children getting colds, the house being untidy, and the fact that the grass grows too quickly.

It's particularly bad during pregnancy and labour. How many dads out there have had the "This is all your fault – don't ever come near me again" speech?

In fact, I might as well take full responsibility now for the Big Bang, the Ice Age, the potato blight of 1854, the Great Fire of London, the Black Death, the collapse of the British Empire, the Wall Street crash, the unacceptably high unemployment rate, and mad cow disease.

Putting it simply, dads get blamed because we're men – and men are responsible for everything that goes wrong. Everything.

Take my wife's squash shorts, for example. When she went to play squash with a friend the other day, she discovered to her horror that her shorts had holes in them.

"You've been using my squash shorts for football, haven't you?" she alleged, opening the case for the prosecution, when I got home from work.

"What are you on about?" I replied.

"They're full of holes. You've been using them for five-a-side and diving around in goal," she persisted.

"Why on earth would I want to wear your squash shorts for football? Everyone would laugh at me," I went on, in desperate mitigation.

"They laugh at you anyway," she cut in, cruelly.

You see, because I'm a dad, and she's a mum, it was like Jack the Ripper trying to drive home his innocence to a judge all too familiar with his previous convictions.

I was no more to blame for the holes in her squash shorts than I am for the hole in the ozone layer, though I bet she has her suspicions about that too. I was totally innocent, yet I'd been found guilty, sentenced and hanged.

A few days later, the chief prosecutor had another court date and went to fetch her squash things from the garage where they are always kept.

It was while she was rooting through her bag that she suddenly came across something which made her go as pale as a judge's wig: **MOUSE DROPPINGS!**

Oh yes, a mouse had eaten my wife's squash shorts and I'd got the blame.

Did I get an apology? Not exactly.

"You must have left the garage door open," she said.

P.S. On the subject of small animals, some people say it's never too early to start encouraging your children to pursue a career. I'm not so sure.

Take the parents of a little girl who wanted to be a vet. They decided to get her a toy vet's kit for her birthday.

It was only when the family cat had to be taken to a real vet to have a plastic thermometer removed from its bottom that they wondered if they'd done the right thing.

A nose for trouble

THERE are some kids who are destined to spend their lives in trouble. Our Jack's one of them. He has an uncanny knack of finding banana skins to slip on. Consequently, he's been a regular at the local hospital in the five eventful years of his life.

Take the last six weeks. First, it was the operation to remove the glass embedded in his foot. A wine glass had been smashed and Jack's foot was drawn to it like a bee to a flower.

Then came the eye patch. He has a lazy left eye, so the hospital decreed that he had to wear a stick-on eye patch for three hours a day over six weeks. He hates it, so to make him feel a bit better, Mum draws an eye on the patch with felt tip pens each day. Jack thinks it makes the patch less obvious. In fact, it makes him look like some kind of Cyclops mutation.

And then came the latest episode in our own running series of Casualty... My wife rang the office to say she'd spent the morning at the hospital. As usual, my blood froze: "What's happened? Is everything OK?"

She'd had a call from school. Jack had been playing with his friend Luke and a button had come off Luke's coat. Jack had walked up to a teacher and announced: "I was just looking at the button and it jumped up my nose."

The teachers couldn't see anything up his nose, but they'd scoured the playground and there was no sign of the button. In the end, it was better to be safe than sorry.

Quite what the hospital staff made of Captain Birdseye Junior arriving with his frantic mother explaining that he had a navy blue button stuck up his nose is anyone's guess.

Once they'd got over the shock, an x-ray confirmed that the button was indeed up his nose and showing no signs of coming down.

They tried everything possible to unbutton him and then a nurse had a brainwave: "Has he had a good blow?" The answer was "no", so one nostril was blocked and he was encouraged to blow as hard as he could through the other.

He took a a deep breath and blew so hard that a gale warning was flashed across the North-East and all shipping was told to head for harbour. But it didn't dislodge the button.

There seemed nothing else for it except general anaesthetic and surgery. But then Jack's luck changed. The blow of blows had made his nose tickle. The tickle turned into a sneeze. And, in a scene reminiscent of Pinnochio being sneezed out of Monstro the whale, the button was fired from his nose like a bullet from a gun.

The next day, I was dragged up to the playground by my one-eyed, button-nosed offspring, shouting: "Quick Dad, there's something I want to show you."

"That's the button that was up my nose," he declared, proudly pointing at Luke's newly-repaired coat...

P.S. Thanks to all those who got in touch after the episode about my little boy having a button stuck up his nose.

It's no laughing matter, but I now know people who've not only had buttons up their nose, but peanuts (chocolate and salted), Lego, pen-tops, and Smarties. I even heard from a woman who'd gone to hospital with a wheel from a model tractor up her hooter.

But my favourite was a man called Mickey Burke, who was travelling to work in Darlington on a bus, idly rolling his ticket between his fingers.

For some unfathomable reason, he poked it deep into his ear. All attempts to get it out failed, so you can imagine his embarrassment when the inspector got on and asked to see his ticket: "I'm sorry, but I've poked it into my ear," said the appropriately named Mr Burke.

He ended up having to get off the bus at Darlington Memorial Hospital so he could report the fact that he had a rolled-up bus ticket stuck in his ear. Thankfully, casualty came to the rescue again.

The things they say...

FOR some reason, we'd had a family trip to a vegetable show in Weardale, and on the way home, five-year-old Jack remarked: "They were the biggest carrots I've ever seen."
Baby Max, who'd been asleep in his car seat, opened one eye and said: "Thomas the Tank Engine's got big carriages."

ANOTHER family trip took us to Redcar Races and my mum was eyeing the runners: "I think I fancy that Beau Roberto," she said.
"You can't," replied an alarmed Hannah, aged seven, " you've got Grandad."

WE were watching James Bond on TV at home..."
Look kids, there's something I've got to tell you," I said. "I'm really a secret agent – I'm 007."
"Yeah," replied our eldest. "That's your IQ."

"MUMMY – I've got a headache in my boppom." – Our two-year-old Max's way of telling us he wants to go to the toilet.

TRIMDON Colliery Brass Band was playing Christmas tunes in Newton Aycliffe and a little boy in a nearby supermarket turned to his mum and said: "I want to go outside and listen to the caramels."

SAM, aged three, from Sunderland, turned to his Auntie Marion and said: "Do you know Auntie Marion, my legs go right up to my bottom."

GARETH, aged three, was with his Mum in Richmond market place when he spotted a woman in a wheelchair with only one leg.
"Mummy," he shouted, "has that lady only got one hole in her knickers?"

"DAD, there's no doubt about it – you're the best hair-washer and Mum's always been the best bum-wiper." – Our Jack, aged six.

"I HATE water – especially really wet water." – Jack again.

"DAD – can I have some money so I can buy you a Father's Day present?" – Another Jack gem.

LEE, seven at the time and living in Loftus, was travelling in the car with his family.
"What are you going to be when you grow up, Lee?" he was asked.
Lee thought for a moment and answered: "I'm going to be a fireman."
"And what qualifications do you think you'll need to do that?" asked his step-dad Simon.
Quick as a flash, Lee came up with the answer: "A pair of wellies and an axe."

Life on the run

RUNNING away from home remains a vivid memory...There'd been some kind of row with my mum and I wanted to really, really punish her.

Dick Whittington must have been fresh in my mind because I prepared for a life on the road by tying a handkerchief to a piece of bamboo cane, stuffing it with custard creams, and stomping off up the road with it slung over my shoulder.

I only got as far as the top of the road. Any further, and I'd have lost sight of the house. So I waited there for what seemed like ages, ate the custard creams, realised a search hadn't been launched, and then went home.

Thirty years on, another runaway drama has unfolded, this time involving our eight-year-old.

It was all caused by the mouse that moved into our garage – the same mouse, you may recall, that got me the blame for making holes in my wife's squash shorts. She'd been convinced I'd been using them for five-a-side football when, in fact, it was the mouse that had been secretly nibbling at them in her sports bag all along.

Anyway, once she'd discovered it was the mouse's fault and not mine, she decided to get a trap.

"It'll have to go – we'll have to kill it," she declared, angrily. I said a little prayer of thanks that I'd been able to divert the blame, and agreed that a trap was the only way.

But the boy has always had a soft spot for animals and swiftly rose to the mouse's defence: "NO! You're not going to kill it – not over my dead body."

Such was the passion of his plea that a compromise was reached. We bought a humane trap which catches them without killing them.

We caught the little blighter at the first attempt. He couldn't resist the piece of cheese we'd left (who could blame him after surviving on a diet of old squash shorts?) and got himself well and truly trapped.

"Ha, ha!" shouted my wife. "That'll teach you to eat my squash shorts." (I considered telling her that she was talking to a mouse but it would have been pointless.)

She announced that 'the guilty one' would be granted his freedom down by the river.

"You can't," bleated the boy. "He needs to go back into the garden so he can return to his wife and his children."

But Mum was having none of that: "He'd come straight back into the garage," she reasoned.

The animal rights protests became louder and louder. The tears flowed. But Mum would not be moved. The mouse was carried to the river, where he shot out of the trap and scurried into the undergrowth.

Mum returned to find the boy filling his backpack with biscuits, a few toys, and his wallet containing £1.14. He ignored all questions, gave her one last, mournful look, and left. He was watched from a discreet distance and we knew he wouldn't be gone long because The Simpsons were due on in half an hour. He was back with minutes to spare.

"Where did you run away to?" I asked him when the drama had subsided.

"Just to the top of the road so I could keep my eye on the house – but don't tell Mum," he whispered. "And, anyway, if she traps any more mice and takes them to the river, I'm going to run away again."

Like the mousetrap, this one could run and run.

Checked your test-tickles lately?

IT'S not really the kind of question you expect when you walk through the door after a hard day's work: "Dad – have you felt your test-tickles today?"

I hadn't as it happened – at least not that I could remember – but my little boy didn't want to let the subject drop: "You have to feel them every day you know Dad, in case you've got test-tickly cancer."

"Oh right," I found myself saying, "I'd better check them straight away then."

"Yep, you might as well," he agreed, before running back into the lounge to watch The Simpsons.

On second thoughts, I decided to have my tea first, and it all became a lot clearer after my wife explained that she'd been given a Department of Health leaflet at school.

Catchily entitled "A Whole New Ball Game", the boy had grabbed it with excitement, thinking it was something to do with football. In fact, it was all about how to check for testicular cancer.

Naturally inquisitive, he'd asked his mum what it was all about and she'd done her best to explain that it was something boys and daddies got and it was important that they felt their testicles regularly to make sure they didn't have any funny lumps on them.

I know from personal experience that testicular cancer is a very serious business.

I have a close friend who found a lump on one of his testicles, but left it for a while before having it checked.

He ended up having to have surgery to have it removed, followed by months of cheomotherapy, and considers himself lucky to be alive.

He was even told he would never have children. But 15 years on, he's a healthy father of three, even though, as he likes to put it, he was "only firing on one cylinder".

Here's some testicular cancer facts:

- It's the most common form of cancer in young men in the UK and occurs mostly in those aged between 19 and 44.
- The risk of developing it has doubled in the past 20 years.
- It is easily treated and if caught at an early stage, it is nearly always curable.
- Only three per cent of young men regularly check their testicles, according to the Imperial Cancer Research Fund.

In our house, the boy didn't need telling twice. In fact, he's been obsessed with making sure his undercarriage isn't lumpy ever since the leaflet arrived.

Mind you, it can be a bit embarrassing, especially if we have company and he's twiddling with them in the kitchen.

"Mum, Mum, do you think this one has gone funny-shaped?" he said the other day, forcing her to break off from cooking his pizza and chips so she could have a look.

"Dad, Dad, I think I've got one test-tickle bigger than the other – what do ya think?" he asked a few days later while he was in the bath.

I'm delighted to report that there's nothing wrong with either of his testicles – or mine for that matter – but we'll go on checking just to be on the safe side.

But what about all you dads out there? Ask yourself this simple question because the answer might just mean that you live old enough to see your kids grow up:

Have you felt your test-tickles today?

- *If you would like to know about testicular or any other kind of cancer, contact the Imperial Cancer Research Fund at PO Box 123, Lincoln's Inn Fields, London, WC2A 3PX.*

Bearing up to life on his own

IT is a defining moment in the lives of all children and their parents – the first school trip.

Our eldest, aged eight, was going away for a whole week.

It was only to York, but it was the first time he'd been away from home and, being a natural worrier, I was a bit anxious.

Memories flooded back from the school trips of my childhood, like the outward bound centre/concentration camp in the Lake District, where my team got hopelessly lost orienteering, and my canoe capsized in ice-cold Coniston.

We'd been asked by the centre leader on the first night if we had an questions: "What happens if we get bitten by an adder in the forest?" I asked as the school's born worrier.

"Die," he replied without a hint of humour.

So who can blame me for being worried now that my little boy was about to shake his feathers and fly the nest for a while?

"Look after yourself and do everything the teachers tell you and remember that we'll be thinking about you," I told him the night before he left.

"Aw shurrup Dad," he replied, pulling a face. "I'm eight you know and I'm not going to miss you one bit. And anyway, I've got a torch in my bag even though we were told not to bring one.

"I can't wait – it's gonna be great. I'm especially looking forward to not seeing Jack for a while."

(Jack's the little brother he pretends to despise.)

Why do they have to grow up so quickly? There he was – seemingly five minutes since he was born – looking forward to being away from us for a week; being all macho and rebellious.

More dads than usual were gathered at the school gates the next morning to see the coach leave. They might have been there simply to make sure they were going to get a week's peace and quiet.

On the other hand, they might have been anxious about getting withdrawal symptoms.

The boys, especially, were high with excitement – running around, playing the fool, making far more noise than was necessary, and then gathering in little whisper-filled huddles. How many more torches were secretly hidden, I wondered.

When the time came for them to leave, I told the boy I was going to miss him and tried to give him a hug.

"Aw Dad, gerrof. I'm going to be OK. I'm eight you know," he squirmed, before marching off defiantly.

But then, when the head-counts had been done and the engine was being revved, he fumbled inside his bag and pulled something out.

It was Winnie, the teddy bear that's been part of his life since he was born. As the bus moved off, it wasn't only the boy who was waving, but Winnie too.

A week might be a long time in politics but it's a good deal longer in parenthood. Although the house was much quieter, the days took an age to pass, and it was great to have him back home. I even got a big hug.

"Did you have a great time?" I asked.

"Yeah, except for two things."

"What were they?"

"Well, the other boys in my room kidnapped Winnie and dangled him out of the window by one of his legs...and I missed you a lot."

Macho, rebellious, growing up. But there's still a long way to go.

Things they don't say...

"We're off to bed early tonight – goodnight everyone."

Nose-picker Nick

There was never a boy with a small finger quicker,
Than Nicholas Watts, the great nostril-picker.
His devilish digit would never stop working,
When his rather large nose told him something was
    lurking.
Like a gun-happy cowboy, quick on the draw,
He'd be there in a flash, it's what fingers are for.
While miners have picks to root out black coal,
Nick's long fingernail scraped his hooter's black
    hole.
When, at last, he succeeded and brought out his
    prize,
He'd flick it at girls, bringing tears to their eyes.
But his mum vowed to be her son's social saviour,
Determined to stamp out such repulsive behaviour.
"If you keep on that picking, I'll stop reading this
    book,"

She told him at bedtime with a withering look.
So Nicholas paused, put his hand by his side,
But in seconds, his finger was back fumbling
    inside.
**"NICK, DIDN'T I TELL YOU, STOP OR I'M
    FINISHED,"**
Screamed his mother, her temper quite
    undiminished.
"But Mummy," said Nick, trying to dodge all the
    flak,
"I wasn't still picking – I was just putting it back!"

- Inspired by a true story of what a little boy
  said to his mum at bedtime.

The things they say...

DAD At Large has often reflected on the dangers of children listening to adult conversations.

The Dad At Large roadshow rolled along to the Eaglescliffe 33 Club and this was a story told by president Margery Britton...

A three-year-old girl from a very nice home was being taught how to save up to open a bank account. Builders were working at the house at the time and the little girl got to know them by helping her mum serve them tea and biscuits.

Occasionally, they would donate five pences to her savings so she found it profitable to hang around and listen to their conversations. Finally she saved up enough and her mum took her to the building society to open her bank account.

"At this rate, you'll be able to open another bank account soon," gushed the cashier.

"Not if the f***** glaziers don't hurry up and get here on time," she replied.

SOMETIMES I worry about our Jack, aged seven. . ."Mum – I know what I want to do when I grow up," he said. "I want world domination."

MUM – you are the leakest wink. Goodbye." – Our Max, aged three.

THE older generation sometimes struggles when it comes to new technology so Jessica, aged seven, was explaining to her grandma how to use a computer.
"Well, you just have to put your hand on the hamster. . ."

The things mums say...

MOVING house is my idea of hell on earth. The removal company had only sent two men to do the moving when we were expecting six. And since we were on an hourly rate, there was nothing else for it – I'd have to join in and help as much as I could.

From 8.30am to 8pm, I humped box after box up and down the stairs.

We finally sat down with a glass of wine at the end of a day which nearly killed me and my wife turned to me and said: "Cor blimey – those two lads worked really hard, didn't they?"

No, she wasn't joking.

"GOODBYE – you're The Weakest Link," – Mum pushing the kids out of the door on the way to school.

The things mums do...

I ALWAYS think you can learn a lot about a woman by what she chooses to stick on her fridge. My wife has just bought a new fridge magnet – it says: "My husband says he'll leave me if I don't stop shopping. Lord I'll miss that man."

Is she trying to tell me something?

JUST in case you think it's only us dads who are useless, there was one member of the Durham County Federation of Women's Institutes – she will remain nameless to save her blushes – who told me how, many years ago, she had been unable to stop her baby crying.
It was only when her husband came home that it was discovered that she'd managed to pin a nappy to the baby's leg!

The square root of all evil

FATHERHOOD was always going to be expensive. But no one warned me I could lose £1m overnight...

Unless you've been living on another planet, you'll have noticed that the country has gone loopy over a TV quiz called 'Who Wants To Be A Millionaire?'

Our kids love it. So much so that they decided we should have a game: "It'll be great, Dad – you can be Chris Tarrant," said our eldest.

Within minutes, two chairs were placed in the middle of the lounge, with 'Chris Tarrant' on one and the other awaiting the first contestant.

The contenders sat on the settee with pens and paper poised as Tarrant posed the question that could earn them a place in the hot seat.

They had to put the following animals in the correct order, from biggest to smallest: a) rabbit b) elephant c) mouse d) rhinoceros.

Predictably, the eldest was quickest with the right answer. His little brother thought the rabbit should come first but he's always been strange.

The successful contestant was shaking with anticipation as he took his place under the lounge light.

It was understandable because he was playing for big money which was due to accumulate with every successful answer: 5p, 10p, 25p, 50p, £1, £1.50, £2, £2.50, £3, £3.50, £4, £4.50, £5. So confident was I that he wouldn't get that far, that the prize jumped to £100,000 at that point and then £1m.

The audience was hushed as the 5p question was asked: How many players in a football team? a)10 b)12 c)11 d)8. Without hesitation, he went for 'c'.

He was up to £3.50 before he needed to use up one of his lives and "ask the audience". Luckily, they confirmed that Rome is indeed the capital of Italy.

He used up another life when he opted for "50-50" on the £5 question: Which part of the body is the tibia? With Mum surreptitiously pointing at her leg, he correctly chose the shinbone.

This was getting serious. Suddenly, it was me who was shaking. Tarrant put on that pseudo-serious smirky look, leaned forward and said: "I can write out a cheque for £5 and you can walk out of this studio a rich man."

"No Dad, sorry Chris, I want to play on," he replied, staring at the floor.

"Sure?"

"I'm sure."

"Absolutely sure?"

"Dad, just get on with it."

"Ok. When did England win the World Cup? a)1962 b)1966 c)1964 d)1960"

"I'll ring a friend," he announced.

He rang Jack Dell, a school friend: "Jack, I'm on 'Who Wants To Be A Millionaire' with my Dad who's Chris Tarrant and I'm ringing a friend – that's you."

Jack was given the four options and went off to check with his Dad. The seconds ticked away: "Come on Jack, come on...pleeeease," whispered the caller.

With five seconds remaining, Jack returned with the correct answer... 1966...£100,000... Oh my God.

He insisted on going for the million. Tarrant had no option but to play dirty:

"The square root of 14,884 – is a) 136, b) 122 c) 143 d) 158."

He protested. He pulled faces. He squirmed in his chair. And, by some astonishing fluke, he guessed right – 122.

For the record, I've written him a cheque for £1m. But, to his dismay, he's banned from cashing it before he's 18.

By then, he'll appreciate it was just a game. Hopefully.

So sorry, Thomas

THOMAS The Tank Engine has been a great friend to me over the past eight years of parenthood.

Each of our four children in close succession has been kept quiet by Thomas videos on mornings when they've woken far too early.

Many is the time I've managed an extra hour's doze on the settee while the little blue puff puff kept them happy until breakfast-time.

Thomas is not just a tank engine. He's a godsend. A hero. A legend. An institution.

And so it is with deep regret that I am now about to insult him...

Our youngest loves Thomas with a passion. He has his stories read to him at bedtime. He watches his videos all day long. He even dreams about him and shouts his name in his sleep.

The only problem is that he can't pronounce his name properly. It comes out as an offensive word which has sadly found its way into the English language.

Forgive me this crudity, but it comes out as Tosser The Tank Engine.

"What story do you want?" I asked him at bedtime the other night.

"Tosser!" he shouted.

"There was no need for that, I was only asking," I felt like saying. But it's not his fault – he's only two and he thinks he's saying Thomas.

The potential for embarrassment is huge. We have to be particularly careful when we're passing toy stores in case he offends any shoppers, and it's a real blessing that he doesn't have any little friends called Thomas.

We did, however, have an awkward moment when I took him down to the local railway bridge to see the trains rushing underneath.

Given that he thinks every choo-choo he sees is Thomas, and that he gets impatient waiting for them, he started shouting for a train to come.

"Tosser, Tosser," he yelled in the loudest voice a two-year-old can muster.

At the very moment he started yelling, a man walking his dog came over the bridge and gave me a very funny look.

And the explanation "Sorry, he's not shouting at you, he's saying Thomas because he wants a train to come" was probably quite meaningless.

The things they say...

A DIVORCED friend of my wife's has a 16-year-old son called David.

David, who lives with his mum, had been round to his dad's house and managed to wangle some money out of him for his holidays.

But David kept it to himself when he also asked his mum for some dosh.

David's sister thought it was only right that their mum was told that David already had some holiday money from his dad.

Angry at the deception, the mum decided to speak to David as soon as he came home from school.

"David, haven't you got something to tell me?"

"No," replied David.

"Oh, I think you have," insisted the mum.

"Alright, alright," said the boy, "I've been going to the pub."

Remember...

IT might be expensive bringing up kids – £20,315 per child for just the first five years, according to a recent survey – but there's always a chance they could grow up to be multi-millionaires, and they're really, really going to owe you.

Me and the blackbird

PARENTHOOD is nothing less than a battle for survival – and us dads have it particularly hard.

Take the blackbird in our back garden as a living example. He and Mrs Blackbird have built a nest in the bush that has grown against the wall of the garage. She duly laid a clutch of eggs and together they've raised four ravenous chicks.

Over the past few weeks, I've watched every day from the kitchen (where I'm usually to be found doing the mountain of washing-up generated by my own four hungry fledglings) as the family 'survival special' has unfolded.

Mr Blackbird has flown himself ragged, back and forth to the nest, with worm after worm in an endless quest to satisfy the four gaping beaks. I would never dream of suggesting that he's henpecked but he's hardly stopped.

And what does Mrs Blackbird do? She sits on the nest, taking it easy. Oh, I've spotted her nipping out now and again but it's probably just to pop over to a friend's nest for the birdie equivalent of a coffee morning.

Through the window, I've developed a real bond with Mr Blackbird. We are birds of a feather: fathers of four; flying around like nobody's business; always being asked for more; knackered.

I have little doubt that Mr Blackbird, after a hard day's worm-hunting, gets kicked out of the nest at night and has to sleep on a spare branch.

It is without question that he has to get up at the crack of dawn because the babies can't sleep and Mrs Blackbird needs a lie-in because her hormones are still recovering.

It is a fair bet that the worms he brings back are never big enough or juicy enough.

And the chances are that one of the chicks throws up over his wing feathers just before he's about to leave for work.

I couldn't help noticing that Mrs Blackbird seems to have an inordinate number of bird

baths in the old watering can while Mr Blackbird never has time.

This week, the young ones finally took flight. The children found one of the baby blackbirds struggling to find its wings under the bush. Concerned for its safety, they ushered it into the flower bed where there was more cover. It is sure to have survived – at least that's what we told the kids.

The next morning – a Sunday full of sunshine promise, the nest definitely empty – I missed seeing my friend the blackbird tirelessly darting around the garden.

And then I spotted him. He was lying on his side with one wing outstretched, as birds sometimes do, sunbathing beneath the apple tree.

Mrs Blackbird was nowhere to be seen. She was probably powdering her beak or having her wings waxed.

"Look at that," I said to my wife. "He must be absolutely shattered, poor thing."

"He'll get eaten by next door's cat if he's not careful," she said, coldly.

She had a point. A blackbird lying on the grass, blinded by the sun, would be easy prey for a merciless predator.

But then I relaxed: "He'll be OK," I replied, wiping the washing-up suds from my hands. "If he can survive bringing up four kids, he can survive anything."

The things they say

THE goodnight telephone call has always had the potential for acute embarrassment...
"Really! You've learned to wee standing up for the first time – aren't you a clever boy," I once found myself saying down the phone in a busy office.

But as the years roll by, it's nice to see other newish dads going through similar humiliations.

I happened to be unashamedly eavesdropping on a goodnight telephone call between a colleague and his little boy the other night.

For reasons best known to the little boy, he has a pet carrot. Not a toy carrot – a real carrot.

The dad didn't know I was listening, and the conversation went along these lines:

"And have you been a good boy for Mummy?

"And did you have a nice time at playschool? That's good.

"No, Daddy doesn't need to say goodnight to the carrot.

"No, honestly, Daddy doesn't need to say goodnight to the carrot. Oh, alright then – put him on.

"Goodnight Mister Carrot, goodnight."

MAX, aged three, was having a cuddle with Mum in our bed on a sunny morning.
Suddenly he got up, went over to the other side of the room, and put his head flat against the wall.
"What are you doing, Max?" asked Mum.
"I'm just seeing if I fit my shadow," he replied.

"DAD – is bloody a square word?" – Max again.

"AW – but I had it first." – Children everywhere.

"AW – do I have to?" – Ditto.

JILL, aged eight, came home from school with a rather delicate question: "How did Mary have a baby without a husband?"
Her Mum did her best to explain: "It was just that God thought she was special."
"No," replied Jill, "I mean Mary, the secretary at school."

Signs of the times

SIGN spotted outside a house in Middleton St George, near Darlington: "Sod the dog – beware the kids."

SIGN spotted outside a house in Neasham, near Darlington: "Beware the wife."

NOTICE outside an amusement park in Birmingham: "Children must be accompanied by daddy and money."

A LITTLE while back, I was reflecting on the growing animosity between our two boys – Christopher and Jack – when they were aged seven and four.
Judging by the sign which was stuck on Christopher's bedroom door a little while later, there doesn't appear to be much chance of significant improvement.
It reads: "JACK FREE ZONE – OFFICIAL"

Unwrapping Cadbury's whole nuts

SOME things are best left to dads...Maureen Brennan is a mum, but she does her best to respond to a crisis. When her 11-year-old daughter Laura came downstairs in tears because her pet hamster – an attractive chocolate-coloured female called Cadbury – had developed a big lump, Maureen tried to stay calm.

She took a good look at Cadbury's lump, decided it was almost certainly terminal, and prepared Laura for the worst.

"Hamsters don't live very long you know," she said, "and there's probably nothing they can do for Cadbury."

Laura, whose mum works behind the bar at Darlington Cricket Club, was very brave. It was decided that if the unthinkable happened, Cadbury would be buried next to Guinness, the family's cat, in her gran's garden in Bishop Auckland.

With heavy hearts, mum, daughter and lumpy hamster, trooped off to the local vet, where the seriousness of the condition warranted an emergency appointment.

The vet – "young and not bad looking" according to Maureen – looked grim as he examined the patient: "Mmm," he said. (It's always bad news when medical people go "Mmm".)

And then, with a sigh, he announced his prognosis: "The lump, Mrs Brennan, is a testicle – you have a healthy MALE hamster."

Whether Cadbury had just the one testicle remains unclear, but a medical record card was duly written out: "No problems – just male," it stated.

Red-faced Maureen had to hand in the card at reception, where she was charged a £5.40 consultation fee by an assistant who couldn't stop laughing.

"Laura got a fit of the giggles too but I had my head in my hands, I was so ashamed," she said.

Word spread quickly. Back at the cricket club, a sign was hung over the bar proclaiming: **"WHAT'S SMALL AND FURRY WITH GROWTHS – DON'T ASK MAUREEN."**

The sign was accompanied by a couple of balloons, though a family column like this would never venture to suggest what they might have symbolised.

It would have been nice to report a happy ending. Sadly, Cadbury died a few weeks later and now occupies the plot in Laura's gran's garden, next to Guinness the cat.

Officially, Cadbury died of natural causes, though it might easily have been acute embarrassment or delayed shock at having his testicles prodded.

Like I said – some things are best left to dads.

Rock and rolling in agony

AN expert on shopping I'm not, but I happen to know there's a chain of stores called 'What Everyone Wants'.

Well, I'm convinced there's a branch out there somewhere called 'Everything Dads Don't Want'.

It must be a goldmine. Mums go there to save shopping around – they can go straight in and be guaranteed of finding presents their husbands won't like.

Obviously, you can't get a Scalextric there, but I imagine the shelves are well stacked with socks.

There'll be plenty of lurid ties, lots of dodgy after-shave and a comprehensive DIY section. Oh, and they apparently sell tickets for Neil Sedaka concerts...

Lots of little things have made me feel old lately: the greying hair; the need to stop wearing contact lenses because my eyes are "drying out"; hearing myself shout at Top of the Pops "Turn that noise down!" just like my dad used to; meeting an old college friend on a train, travelling to his daughter's graduation.

But nothing – I mean nothing – made me feel quite as old as getting tickets to a Neil Sedaka concert for my 37th birthday.

Let me explain... When I was a boy, I got a job helping deliver potatoes for a local farmer. It only lasted a day because I accidentally left the back doors of his van open, sending a spud avalanche rolling down Bevanlee Road in South Bank, Middlesbrough.

There was a steel strike going on, times were hard, and I can still see people running from their homes to gleefully collect their free King Edwards before nipping back inside to put the chip pan on.

My wages were consequently docked from a fiver to £3 but it was just enough to buy my first LP – a Neil Sedaka compilation. 'Oh Carol' was a hit at the time and it seemed like a good idea.

It is because that dog-eared old album has been part of my record collection ever since, that my wife decided tickets to see Neil Sedaka at Newcastle City Hall would be appreciated.

It was one those moments when you open your present, try desperately to hide your disappointment and say: "Lovely."

Neil is on his 'Celebration Tour' because he's been in the business for 40 years and he's 60 this year, although his dazzling teeth and shiny black hair are a lot younger.

I did my best to keep the concert date quiet – it's not good for a rock 'n roll child's image to go to a Neil Sedaka concert – but word seeped out.

My heart sank further on the approach to the City Hall when we passed a couple of elderly fans having sandwiches and a flask of tea in their car.

Inside the venue, it was a blue rinse ocean.

But honesty is everything and it is my duty to report that Mr Sedaka was fantastic, belting out classics like Calendar Girl, Happy Birthday Sweet Sixteen, Solitaire, Laughter in the Rain (my favourite) and Tillie the Twirler.

It was during Tillie The Twirler that my back went. The City Hall's a great venue apart from the fact that the seating has been arranged for sardines.

As I tried to extricate my legs to go to the loo, I cried out in pain so loud that Neil must have thought I was harmonising. I've been in agony with a trapped nerve ever since.

People have been asking how it happened and I've simply had to say: "Sorry, it's too embarrassing."

They immediately think it's something to do with sex. (Chance would be a fine thing). Anyway, I'd be grateful if you don't let on.

Things they say...

"IT must be my turn for the bath tonight."

Thomas and Percy in train disaster

BEING a dad is like starring in one long episode of Casualty – especially when you've got as many kids as me.

The hospital dramas began with the most frightening – an emergency operation to clear our baby girl's blocked intestine when she was just months old.

Since then we've had the poisoned finger, the broken glass in the foot, the perforated eardrum, the eye infection, and the button stuck up the nose to name but a few.

But the latest is possibly the most delicate. It shall be recorded for posterity as the 'todgy in the train set incident'.

Naturally, it had to happen two days before our long-awaited, 'relaxing' family holiday. Our two-year-old was playing, happily and naked, on the floor with his little 'Tosser' train set. (He still can't pronounce Thomas.)

Suddenly, he began to scream. We thought he'd caught his finger in the track which folds in on itself and snaps shut.

But he hadn't – he'd trapped the end of that private and highly sensitive part of the male anatomy which is known in our house as Mister Todgy.

Panic set in. Mister Todgy was bleeding, starting to swell and pointing in a funny direction. A call to the doctor's surgery directed us straight to hospital.

"Surname?" asked the receptionist at accident and emergency.

"Barron."

"Christian name?"

"Max."

"Date of birth?"

"28th of March, 1997."

"What's happened to him?"

"Little Percy got trapped in his Thomas train set."

"Sorry?"

"He's caught his todgy – penis – in the track of his train set and it's bleeding, swelling and pointing to the left. Thought we'd better come in to be on the safe side."

"Oh. Right. I'll take you straight down."

I didn't argue. It was a packed waiting room and they were all looking at me as if I'd just landed from a different planet.

The doctor came in, looking worried, and accompanied by a nurse: "Well, we've not had one of these before – can you take his nappy off please?"

By now, the affected area was as red as a stop signal and swollen to the kind of proportions I wouldn't have been ashamed of.

"I'm going to have to have a close look," said the doctor.

The baby wasn't at all keen to co-operate – well, would you be if you'd had your todgy trapped in a train set?

He kicked and screamed, the nurse held his legs, and I held his arms while telling him to look at the lovely pictures on the wall: "Oh look, there's one of Tosser," I shouted desperately.

The nurse and doctor glanced up at each other. He went back to shining a torch at Mr Todgy and declared he needed a second opinion.

Another doctor came, and we went through the same rigmarole until we were given the verdict: he should be OK but it was a near miss and he'd need strong pain-killers and antibiotics for a week.

"If it gets infected or he has trouble passing water, come straight back," instructed the second doctor.

"We're going on holiday," I explained.

"Well, check that there's a hospital close by."

It had better have a nervous breakdown clinic because I'm in danger of going off the rails.

The things dads say (and do)

HARRY Nancarrow was a Mosquito pilot and a veteran of 50 wartime operations.

He was also a loving dad and clearly a quick-witted one at that.

His son Anthony is grown-up now, but when he was a little lad, he turned to his dad and said: "Dad, when you fought in the war, did you fight the Romans?"

"No son, Pontius was the pilot in those days," said Harry, quick as a burst of machine gunfire.

Harry died recently. Many thanks to his widow Margaret, of Shadforth, near Durham, for telling me this story.

IT'S hard when you're a dad having to come to terms with middle-age.

A father-of-two I know was getting increasingly conscious of his greying hair so he decided to take drastic action with a bottle of dye.

Naturally, he had to take a fair amount of ribbing over his new chestnut-brown locks, not least from me.

"Look," he protested, "I dyed it grey and I didn't like it so I've let it grow back to its natural colour."

THERE I was, having a shower after a tough session in the gym.

A bloke came in and I heard him curse to himself before he walked over, stark naked, and said: "Excuse me mate, I couldn't have a bit of shampoo could I?"

"Sure – no problem," I said, a little nervously, before letting him have a squirt of my Wash 'N Go, and sincerely wishing he would.

"I brought the wrong bottle," he explained, "this is the oil for the baby's nappy rash."

RONNIE Angel, a bricklayer living in Norton, Stockton, was tired after a day at work.

His daughter Doreen loved nothing more than plaiting hair – whether it was her own or her dolls'.

Seeing her dad snoozing in the chair, she couldn't resist putting lots of bright red bows in his hair.

A little while later, there was a knock at the door and Ronnie woke with a start.

He jumped up to answer the door and couldn't understand why he was getting such a strange look from the bloke on the doorstep.

AND here's another little tale which underlines just how much pain us dads go through...

The Dad At Large tour had reached the welcoming home of the Bondgate Methodists Women's Fellowship in Darlington.

Two of the members, Barbara and Fay, were in fits as they recalled the day their husbands went to Darlington Memorial Hospital together to have vasectomies.

As they emerged from the hospital with the job done, the ordeal finally became too much for Fay's husband and he collapsed in a heap.

Barbara's husband, as any friend would, bent down to pick him up – and promptly burst his stitches.

Both ended up back in hospital for a little more treatment.

And I bet neither got any sympathy.

The Horse of the Rear Show

"DAD, we're bored. What can we do? Think of something Dad – quickly."

Dads are expected to be good at coming up with ideas during the long – too long – summer holidays.

The holidays were almost over and I'd just about run out of ideas. And then I remembered – the Space Hopper Horse of the Year Show. Of course, why hadn't I thought of it before?

It was a memory dredged up from childhood. We used to set up a show-jumping course in the garden – using anything we could find – and compete against the clock on a Space Hopper.

We even taped the music from the real Horse of the Year Show and played it as we bounced round the course, getting four faults for every fence we failed to clear. Three decades on, a new Space Hopper was collected from its stable (the garage) and brought into the arena.

The course was demanding to say the least: The first fence was the tennis net, lowered to an acceptable level. The second was the sweeping brush. The third was made up of two rows of clothes pegs with a blanket in the middle. The fourth was the real tester. A sharp turn into the water-jump – a washing-up bowl filled with cold suds from when we'd washed the car earlier. If you cleared that, it was on to the fifth and final fence – Mum's washing basket – and a dash for the finish.

Hannah, aged seven, went first. We decided she was Lucinda Prior-Palmer riding a 'horse' called Pixie. Dad provided the commentary...

"And the arena's hushed as Lucinda Prior-Palmer on her lovely orange horse Pixie gets ready to go...and she's off...and, yes, she's over the tennis net without any trouble...and she's easily cleared the sweeping brush...and she's going like the clappers towards the clothes pegs and...oh what a leap...and she's lost no time on the turn...and here's the water jump...and she sails over...and can she clear the washing basket?...the answer's an emphatic 'yes'...and it's a spectacular clear round in just 24 seconds. Fantastic!"

Jack, aged five, went next – Harvey Smith on 'Bouncer'.

"And here we have Harvey Smith, looking a little nervous on Bouncer who's on his toes...and they're away...and, whoops, it's four faults at the net...and up to the brush...and, whoops, it's another four faults...and can he get over the pegs...and, whoops, it's another four faults...that's 12 altogether...and he's having trouble controlling Bouncer who seems to have a mind of his own...and the water jump's the other way Harvey...and oh my goodness me...what a disaster."

Bouncer had finally regained his sense of direction, approached the water jump, took an enormous bounce, flew from between his rider's legs, and left hapless Harvey sitting in the washing-up bowl.

Lucinda – once she'd finished laughing – performed another immaculate round in 22 seconds while Harvey, dripping wet, went off to change.

He emerged seconds later – stark naked. Lady Godiva must have been turning in her grave as he bounced cheekily round the garden, giggling like mad, and hitting every fence in sight on a mount we decided had to be called Streaker. The Horse of the Year had turned into The Horse of the Rear Show.

The water jump went everywhere and Mum's washing basket was squashed by a muddy Space Hopper.

Let's just say if it hadn't had some clean washing in it, I might not have been in for the high jump...

Caught at silly point

IT was a simple enough request: "Dad, will you get the cricket set down from the loft?"

A friend had passed on the cricket set a few years ago – bat, ball, stumps, bails, gloves, pads and a "box" – but the kids had been too small to make use of it.

A box, for the uninitiated, is something designed to protect the batsman from getting a very hard ball in the nether regions, which can be every bit as painful as a vasectomy.

Happy that they'd remembered the gift, I was halfway up the ladder when Mum shouted: "You can't go up there – there's a wasp's nest."

She'd seen wasps going in and out under the eaves and had heard them buzzing overhead but decided to wait until they died in the cold weather so the children could take the nest into school.

"Oh, I'll be OK," I said, hesitantly climbing another rung.

"You're not going up there – you'll get stung to bits," she insisted. (It's times like these that remind you that you are loved after all.)

I climbed down, apologising to our eldest for not being able to fetch the cricket set.

The initial look of disappointment on his face was swiftly replaced by a smile which suggested he'd had a bright idea.

Seconds later, he was back with his sister and little brother: "Look Dad, we've brought you something to protect you from the wasps. Put this on," he said, handing me a raincoat.

Grinning with excitement, they ran off again and returned with a pair of dirty old gardening gloves: "And this will make sure your hands are safe."

Off they went again and came back with a yellow scarf: "We don't want those naughty wasps to get down your shirt, do we?" said my little girl.

A woolly hat came next. It was a nice, calm, sunny day outside but I looked like I was ready to face Hurricane Floyd.

"Hold on, what about my face?" I asked.

"Mmmm. That's a tricky one," said the eldest. "Got it – wait there."

They all vanished and could be heard in deep conversation in the kitchen.

They reappeared with a large sieve: "There you go, Dad. Tuck the handle inside the scarf to hold it over your face."

So there I was, looking like a cross between an Arctic explorer and Hannibal Lecter. Nervously, looking stupid, and sweating profusely, I climbed the ladder to the loft and peered in.

I could see the cricket set against the far wall. There was no sign of 'the enemy' but they might strike at any moment.

My heart pumping, I scrambled across the loft floor like lightning, grabbed the cricket set and dived back towards the ladder. I think I saw some wasps coming after me but I can't be sure. It's not easy to see anything through a sieve, especially when it's still dusted with flour.

"Thanks Dad – you're a real hero," said the eldest, sincerely.

"Yeah, Dad, you're a real hero," added my wife, sarcastically.

It had all been worth it as far as I was concerned. It would be good to hear the sound of leather on willow in the back garden.

The thought was interrupted by our five-year-old appearing at the door, with the box strapped onto his head.

"Hey, thanks, Dad – great sword fencing hat," he said.

A taste of his own medicine

POETIC justice is a wonderful thing...Three years ago, my eldest had a pirate party for his sixth birthday. The coup de grace was that I – dressed as Captain Hook – had to be tied to the garage door and have water bombs thrown at me by dozens of little pirates.

The soaking itself lasted about 20 minutes. The subsequent flu lasted around 10 days. I wouldn't be surprised if it was pneumonia but I don't want to be accused of being a hypochondriac. (Everyone knows that dads are more susceptible to viruses than mums, and that they feel pain more acutely but it's never publicly acknowledged.)

Nevertheless, the party is remembered as a great success. So much so that when 'number three' celebrated his sixth birthday at the weekend, he decided he wanted a pirate party just like his big brother's.

The dreaded day dawned and there I was again, spending the morning filling balloon after balloon with ice cold water.

The pirates arrived one by one with their hats, eye patches, striped shirts, rolled-up trousers, swords, hooks and "oo-ah-me-hearties" (and that was just the dads).

The first job was the scars. Any self-respecting pirate needs a decent scar so I spent the first half an hour creating horrible, gaping wounds with my face-painting set.

"Can I have one right down my leg so it looks like a sword's chopped it down to the bone and it's gone all poisony," said one little pirate, cheerfully.

"Course you can," I said. "One gangrenous leg coming up."

"No," replied the pirate, "I just want a big scar."

They searched for hidden treasure. They played 'pin the patch on the pirate' and I'll never forgive the little so and so who said "that pirate's got one arm longer than the other". It took me hours to draw that pirate.

They played 'pop the pirate balloon with a sword while blindfolded' and I'm a lucky dad to have emerged with all my faculties intact.

Finally, it was time for the grand finale – the water bombs. There was a frenzy of excitement as I was manhandled into position.

The first balloon exploded against the wall behind me and the water trickled down my back. The second was a direct hit. So was the third. The fourth splattered at my feet and the water splashed up the legs of my shorts. And so it went on.

Eventually, everyone had thrown a bomb each and there were two left. Someone handed one to my wife and, for reasons I can't fathom, she accepted with the kind of glint in her eye I haven't seen since she packed me off for my vasectomy. It hit me smack in the face and she danced with joy.

"Can I have the last one?" It was the voice of our eldest – the one who'd started it all with his own pirate party three years ago.

He picked up the last, bloated, blue balloon with the smile of a cruel assassin.

He lifted it above his head – **AND IT BURST!**

He was left dripping and spluttering and everyone was laughing at him instead of me.

Thank you, Lord, thank you.

The things they say

"THE Easter bunny came when I was in the creche, but I know it was a human inside and humans can't lay eggs." – Our Max, aged four.

A FELLOW dad has been telling me how his little lad had everyone in fits at the local chip shop.
This particular family keeps hens and Dad was making idle conversation with the staff behind the counter.
"Weather's mild," he said. "So mild we're getting an egg a day out of the hens."
"Aye," the little lad chipped in, "and, if they don't, we just squeeze their bums."

"LITTLE Miss Muffet sat on a tuffet, eating her curtains away." – Our two-year-old Max.
It's probably just as well the spider frightened Miss Muffet away, otherwise she'd have ended up looking really drawn. . .

WHEN she was a little girl, Gillian Ashton, of Coulby Newham, near Middlesbrough, was all excited about being enrolled in the Brownies: "Mummy, Mummy," she shouted, "I've been embalmed."

TOM, aged six, who has decided he's "only writing to Santa on the off-chance he still exists" spent the week practising getting up at 4am on Christmas Day.
He feels this gives him more time to play with his presents and therefore he "won't have to rush at everything".

MY little girl Hannah, aged five: "Dad, is it true that you get square eyes if you watch too much tellyvizzen?"
Me: "Yes, it is."
Hannah: "Good – I'll be able to see round corners and check what Jack's up to in my room."

"DAD, I saw an accident once and some paraletics turned up in an ambulance." – Our five-year-old Jack. I think he meant paramedics but it's hard to be sure.

CHARLIE Weir, aged ten, from Darlington, was discussing the Olympics with his mum.
"I hope Redgrave and Pinsent win," she said.
"Are they in the cockless fours?" asked Charlie.

FOUR-year-old Helen Dawber, of Seaton Carew, was having a philosophical discussion with her grandma...
Grandma: "You'll have to put your thinking cap on, Helen."
Helen: "I haven't got a thinking cap Grandma – but I have got a baseball cap."

A brush with disaster

SOME things are best left to mums. Like decorating and potty training.

Sorry, but I'm no good at either. It all just ends up as one big horrible mess if I get involved.

But my wife, God bless her, is brilliant at both. She's had her hands full in the last week or so, decorating the downstairs toilet and desperately trying to coax our two-year-old out of nappies.

"Are you going to show Mummy what a big boy you are?" I heard her say the other day. For one glorious, fleeting moment, I thought she was talking to me, but then I realised she was addressing 'the little un' with a pair of pants in her hands.

If we can get him out of nappies and into 'big boy's pants' we can get him into the local playgroup and, since he's the last of four, finally stop shelling out a small fortune on disposables.

"No more nappies, no more nappies, no more nappies, no more nappies."

I can apparently be heard saying it over and over again in my sleep.

To begin with, he got caught up in the general enthusiasm of the rest of the family, who gave him a rapturous round of applause and took him on a lap of honour every time he squeezed a couple of miserly drips into the shiny blue potty.

But to be truthful, the successes were hardly worth talking about. Most of the time, he'd go through his nappyless days weeing in the paddling pool, in the bath, in the garage, in the plant pots – anywhere, in fact, except in the potty.

In the end, he got bored with the whole thing and stopped making any effort, insisting that he didn't want to use the potty because "I not a big boy, I still a ickle baby."

The ickle baby nappies returned and the big boy's pants were put away for a while, but Mrs Dad At Large is nothing if not persistent.

She kept on telling him about all the wonderful things he'd be able to do once he was a big boy: He'd be able to go to playgroup; he could sit in a big boy's booster seat in the car; he wouldn't have to sit in a high-chair at the table; and Daddy might take him to see a proper football match with the others.

"Me not need a nappy now – me going to be a big boy," he proclaimed, instantly persuaded. The nappy was duly whipped off again and Mum got on with the decorating as best she could with her fingers crossed.

The toilet door, having been given a nice fresh coat of paint, was propped open with her shoe to dry, and she nipped into the garage to mix some more paint.

Suddenly, the little 'un rushed in, dancing and shouting with great excitement: "Me hab a wee. Me hab a wee. Me a big boy. Me a big boy. Me hab a big wee."

"Oh well done," said Mum, following him eagerly towards the toilet so she could admire his achievement. "Have you used the potty like a big boy?"

"No, no,' he answered proudly, pointing to the floor. "Me done it in your shoe."

Like I said, some things are best left to mums. And I have to say, she's made a lovely job of that toilet...

Things they don't say...

"I'VE tidied my room and put everything away neatly. Is there anything else I can do to make your life easier?"

"NO, it's OK, Dad, I don't need any pocket money this week."

Lessons in thuggery

WHY? Why should one child want to be violent to another just because of the colour of his football shirt?

Our eldest, aged nine, had reached a defining moment in his life: "Dad, I've decided to be a goalkeeper just like you – it must run in the blood," he'd told me, smiling with excitement.

Like me, he may well have been forced into this momentous decision because he's no good at scoring, tackling, running, defending, passing or dribbling.

His pronouncement coincided with a leaflet from Darlington Football Club arriving at his school, promoting a football coaching programme, including a two-day goalkeepers' course.

"Can I go Dad, can I, can I. It's only £5."

The boy looked forward to it for a week and we practised crosses and dives so much that the back garden developed a bald patch to rival my own and the washing machine worked overtime.

When the big day dawned, he dug out his David Seaman goalie shirt and we set off with dreams of Wembley in our heads.

He was duly signed on the register and he ran off to have a preliminary kick around with a gang of other kids who were waiting on the muddy pitch for the course to begin.

I stood on the touchline, glowing with pride that he had the confidence to go and introduce himself to a bunch of kids he'd never met before.

It was then that it happened. One of the boys walked over and elbowed him in the stomach.

The red mist descended. Overcome with anger and disbelief, I sprinted over and shouted at the other boy: "What did you do that for?"

"What?" he replied, with mock innocence.

"Leave it Dad, leave it," protested the injured party.

"*You* know what – what did you thump him for?" I persisted.

"Cos he's got an Arsenal shirt on. Don't like Arsenal," he mumbled.

It was only then that I noticed he was wearing a Manchester United shirt. Before elbowing my son, he'd gone up to him and said: "We don't want Arsenal supporters on this course so **** off."

Why?

The unsavoury incident was sorted out by the organisers and our would-be David Seaman thoroughly enjoyed the course, although he was forced to admit: "I think I have a bit of a problem with catching the ball." (It does run in the blood.)

A few days later, we were going somewhere in the car and Mum was complaining about the fact that she hadn't had time to do her hair properly.

"Don't worry Mum," said Young Seaman, you don't have to take insults from anyone – that's what I always tell myself when I'm wearing my Arsenal shirt."

That night, me and the kids settled down for our usual Saturday night treat – watching Match of the Day. Mum goes to bed to read and we push the settee up close to the telly, turn the lights out, snuggle up under duvets and eat crisps while we watch the footie – just like I used to when I was little.

Middlesbrough were playing Sunderland. It was dominated by players – earning tens of thousands of pounds a week – screaming, glaring, and swearing at the referee every time a decision went against them.

And then, when the referee wasn't looking, a Middlesbrough player was caught on camera, deliberately elbowing an opponent in the face, sending him sprawling on the turf, and pretending he hadn't done a thing.

Then I remembered why children behave like little hooligans.

Trust me

HOW come mums think dads are useless? They treat us as if we have just one brain cell to share around between us.

Take last weekend. My wife and a dozen or so girlfriends decided they deserved a break and went away to a health spa for a few days.

A week earlier, as we stood watching footie practice, us dads discussed the potentially horrifying prospect of being 'home alone'...

"Don't know what all the fuss is about – I'll just take them to me mam's," said one.

"Aye," we all nodded in acknowledgement of a well thought out tactic.

To say my wife doesn't trust me is an understatement: "Are you going to be OK?" she kept asking.

"Look, stop worrying. I can handle four kids," I kept saying. "Just you have a nice, relaxing time – you deserve it." (Bit of slavver – another sound tactic.)

The notices went up the day before her departure. Huge sheets crammed with instructions – an idiot's guide to looking after four kids aged nine, seven, six and two – stuck to the kitchen walls. To be frank, it was an insult. These are merely extracts:

Friday

"By 8.55am: Take kids to school.

By 11am: Take lovely wife to meet other girls for journey to health spa.

11.15am: Come home and clear up kitchen. Tidy round. Open curtains. Make beds (do this every day).

3.15pm: Collect kids from school.

5pm: Feed them.

Saturday

10am: Take Christopher to football practice.

11am Pick him up from football practice.

12am: Do them some lunch.

2pm: Take them to village Christmas fair.

Sunday

Your own day to plan but ensure they're fed.

Monday

Before going to school: Put out bins.

By 8.55am: Take kids to school again (Don't forget packed lunches – see additional notes on pantry door).

9.30am: Take Max to play school.

11.45am NO LATER: Pick up Max from play school.

The rest of the day should be spent running around like something demented, tidying up real good for me coming home."

I was hurt but I tried not to show it. It was insulting but useful too. After dropping off the kids at school, I even made her a nice going-away breakfast to show there were no hard feelings.

"Are you going to turn the grill off, or are you just going to let the house burn down?" she asked as we were about to leave. "Are you sure you're safe to be left?"

"I'll be fine," I replied, turning off the grill.

"Oh, and don't worry your pretty little head about the washing – it's all done," she added, with one last, patronising, sexist flourish.

We drove to her friend's house where the spa-ing partners had arranged to meet. You should have seen how many bottles of wine they'd packed.

"Are you sure you'll be alright?" she asked for the 152nd time as I gave her a hug.

"Trust me – nothing will go wrong," I promised.

She got out, walked down the drive and disappeared inside the house with a wave.

I sighed, reflected on her lack of confidence in me, put the gear-stick into reverse, began to mentally unravel the jumble of things I had to do, and – **CRUNCH!** – backed straight into a parked car.

For the record, the accident has been properly reported, though not yet to my wife – she'd have only worried that I wasn't safe to be left on my own.

Left feeling a right drip

IT is a heartening sign as we approach the new millennium that women are at last starting to show a little more understanding about the plight of us dads.

Several messages of sympathy were gratefully received following my last column, recounting how my wife and 12 other mums from our village went off to a health spa for a long weekend, shamelessly leaving us dads on our own with the kids.

I had mums come up to me at the school gates on the Monday after my ordeal, lay their hands gently on mine and say things like: "Did you manage OK?"

One, whose sincerity is not in question, shouted across the playground: "You look really tired – it must have been awful for you having to cope all on your own. You're very brave."

Indeed I was. I'd kept telling my wife that there was nothing to worry about and I would argue that I did rather well. Apart from…

- Crashing the car within seconds of dropping her off because my head was so full of instructions.
- Microwaving the pizza on 'defrost' rather than full power.
- Our two-year-old deciding to drop my glasses down the toilet and telling me "It's a good game isn't it?" when I asked him why he'd done it.
- The same little horror having a spectacular setback in his potty training.
- And the fact that I had to fill the bath with a kettle.

The bathtime problem wasn't my fault anyway. As I explained last time round, my wife – thinking that I'm stupid – had left huge sheets of instructions pinned up all over the house.

There were detailed notes on what time I had to take them to school, what I had to put in their packed lunches, what time I had to pick them up, directions to where all their clothes were kept, what to do in emergencies, and how I wasn't to forget to feed them.

All very useful. But where oh where were the instructions on how to get hot water?

When it came to bath time on Sunday night, there was no hot water left and I was left helpless. What's the point of an idiot's guide to looking after kids if it is so fundamentally flawed?

I've never had to know before because there's always been hot water in the tap whenever I've turned it on. But, in her wisdom, she'd decided to keep the location of the magic emersion switch to herself.

I hunted high and low but couldn't find it anywhere. In the end, there was nothing else for it but to trek up and down the stairs 533 times with a kettle.

I was all ready to give her a piece of my mind when she got home, but I suppose everyone makes mistakes.

And anyway, she was too busy hugging the kids to have taken any notice.

They were pleased to see her too. They'd even made her a card: "Welcome home," it said. "Dad's been quite a good Mum, but not as good as you."

Next time, I'll make them have cold baths.

A white Christmas lie

IT is a question every child asks sooner or later – and one that every parent has to face up to: Does Father Christmas really exist?

I was only seven when my older brother took me to one side and made me cry by whispering: "It's not true you know – Santa's just made-up. Mum and Dad bring the presents."

Naturally, I didn't believe him any more than I had when he alleged that Batman and Robin weren't real either. How ridiculous. After all, if Batman and Robin didn't exist, The Penguin and The Joker would have ruled the world, wouldn't they?

Nevertheless, my big brother's cruel claims knocked the Christmas stuffing out of me all those years ago.

This year, our eldest is nine – he's so big I can barely lift him, let alone carry him on my shoulders like I used to.

And the questions are coming as thick as Santa's beard and as fast as Rudolf across the rooftops. It's touch and go whether he still believes.

It gained momentum when we were decorating the tree and he found a white beard in the bottom of the decorations box: "What's this Mum?" he asked, holding it up, accusingly.

"Er, nothing," she said, grabbing it off him. The inquest into how it got left there is still to be held.

It was the following morning before the boy pushed it further: "Mum, is it Dad or one of his friends who's been dressing up as Santa?"

"Don't be silly – oh look, it's starting to snow," she replied.

The boy, under pressure from a growing number of disbelievers at school, is caught in that classic trap of doubting that Santa exists but not wanting to say so out loud in case it means he doesn't get any presents.

It finally all got too much for him at the end of the school holidays. He got me on my own, looked me in the eye and said: "Dad, I need to talk to you. Now tell me the truth because they're all saying it at school."

"Saying what?"

"Saying that Santa doesn't exist and that you and Mum bring all the presents. Dad, just tell me it straight. I'm nine now and I have a right to know."

I thought of all the times I'd watched his face light up when Santa had emerged from the shadows and bellowed "Ho, ho ho" in his bedroom.

I thought of all the letters he'd sent to the North Pole, asking for all kinds of things in handwriting that became gradually more legible as the years passed by.

I thought about the times he'd left Santa sausage rolls and glasses of wine on the mantelpiece, and filled buckets of water to be left under the tree for Rudolf.

I thought about the time as a toddler he couldn't pronounce his s's and he'd told Santa that Daddy wanted a pair of nice, warm 'flippers' for Christmas.

But, like I said, the question has to be faced by us all sooner or later. Children grow up quicker than any of us would like and, in the end, the truth just has to be told.

And so, with a little lump in my throat, I looked him in the eye, held him by the shoulders, and quietly told him what he needed to know: "Father Christmas, he…well, he…he really does exist."

Things they don't say...

"DAD, any chance of some more sprouts – they're really yummy."

The things they say

KEITH and Lucy Teasdale told me in Bishop Auckland about how their son Craig had reacted when his expectant mum asked if he wanted a baby brother or sister: "Can't we have a rabbit?"

"DADDY, Aladdin's trying to get a piggy back again off Jasmine. He likes piggy backs, doesn't he Dad?" - Our Jack, aged an innocent six. (Jasmine and Aladdin were, of course, our pet rabbits.)

ASA, aged three, had just come home from nursery. He turned to his mum to ask about a new song he'd been learning: "Mum – who is Dougie Hokey Cokey?"

"Dad, can I have something to mop up with?" asked three-year-old Max.
"Why, what have you done?" I enquired with a sigh I've sighed a million times before.
"It's a secret – but it's on the lounge carpet," he answered.

Our Max, aged three, had come home from nursery with a special Mother's Day present – a necklace made out of pasta tubes.
"Oh Max, it's lovely," cooed his mum. "It was made with love, wasn't it?"
"No," replied Max firmly, " it was made with pasta."

THANK you to Susan Whittle, of Tudhoe Village, County Durham, who sent me a letter about her little boy Daniel. Daniel, aged six, had found a woodlouse in the house. After returning it safely to the garden, he turned to his mum and said: "Mummy, if it had been a Millennium ant, you would have killed it wouldn't you, because they can damage electrical wires and things."

MY mate John has a little boy who's discovered Toy Story.
Bemused by Buzz Lightyear's phrase 'To Infinity and Beyond', the boy asked his dad: "What does infinity mean?"
"Well," said his dad, somewhat tentatively, realising that even the likes of Einstein and Hawking had struggled with that one, "It's like this... er....um..."
Dad, desperate not to lose face, had a brainwave: "You know how our road has a wall at the end," he said, gaining confidence as he rewrote the laws of physics, "well infinity is like our road but without the wall at the end."
A few minutes later, smug dad and young son went out in the car.
"Dad," asked his son, looking out of the window, "are those gardens infinity?"
"What?" asked his puzzled dad. "It's just that they haven't got any walls either," said the boy.
Dad decided to stick to the simple stuff after that.

Mums never forget

SOMETIMES, I seriously worry about Santa. I know he's been around a long time, and he has a lot on his mind over Christmas, but I think he's losing his memory.

He arrived at our house at around 8pm on Christmas Eve, looking suspiciously like my mate Nigel. He had his glass of Baileys, and went upstairs where four of his biggest fans were waiting for him, trembling with excitement.

"Ho, ho, ho. Merry Christmas," he boomed. "What would you like me to bring you then?" he asked, sitting down next to Christopher, the eldest, who's been wavering as a believer.

"Just two things please Santa – world peace and a Pokemon computer game."

"I'll see what I can do. And what about you?" he asked Hannah, seven.

"A Shania Twain CD please," she replied. For those unfamiliar with the sounds in the hit parade these days, Shania Twain is a singer – and a very attractive one at that, with a splendid figure and long, shimmering dark hair.

"Mmmm," said Santa, stroking his beard, innocently, "I'm not sure, but I think I had Shania Twain on my sleigh earlier."

I couldn't help thinking that if Santa did have Shania Twain on his sleigh, he'd have jolly well remembered. I know I would have done. But you see what I mean about his memory?

And I was really relying on him this year because – for the tenth Christmas in a row – I'd asked him to bring me a Scalextric.

My wife had always put him off before, arguing that the kids weren't old enough to look after a Scalextric, which completely missed the point because it had nothing whatsoever to do with them.

But this year, there were lots of little hints

that my wish might finally come true. So it was with excitement fluttering in my heart that I finally went to bed on Christmas Eve, still giggling at the vision of Shania and Santa on the sleigh.

Actually, it was Christmas Day when we got to bed because it was 1.30am by the time we'd finished wrapping things.

It was just after 5am when the kids appeared at our door, holding their stockings, and shouting **"MUM, DAD – HE'S BEEN! CAN WE GO DOWNSTAIRS? CAN WE? CAN WE?"**

I didn't mind too much because I couldn't wait to unwrap *you know what*. Imagine my disappointment when I opened my presents to discover a new wedding ring to replace the one I'd lost two years ago (she didn't talk to me for ages), an Elvis Costello CD, and a Billy Connolly video.

Naturally, I pretended to be pleased and the day passed reasonably happily, but I was still feeling deflated on Boxing Day when we went over to Grandma and Grandad's house.

The kids opened yet more presents and then Grandma handed me a package. My heart jumped momentarily but I could feel from the paper that it was just another shirt. Oh well, maybe next year.

But then she handed over another one, saying: "Here – that one's for you and Jack to share."

It was big. It was in a box. Me, aged 37, and Jack, aged six, tore the paper off voraciously. And there it was – my (our) very own Scalextric, with a red Ferrari car and a green Benetton rival.

Well, I could have cried. You might not be able to depend on Santa anymore – but you can always rely on your dear old mum not to forget her little boy.

Grand prix disaster

THIS is a real life tale – or tail – with a rather shocking ending. So be warned.

Last time round, I was delighted to announce that Santa had finally made my wish come true and brought me a Scalextric for Christmas.

It seems lots of other dads got Scalextrics too because several of them called to share in the excitement. It doesn't take much to keep us happy.

But Scalextrics can apparently be dangerous. Oh yes – they can be the pits if you're not careful.

A true story reached me, amid all the Scalextric mania, about a little boy who lives in a village near Darlington. He and his dad are the proud owners of a Scalextric, just like me and our Jack.

The boy, known only as David to save his blushes, was seven at the time and was playing with his Scalextric in his bedroom.

(His dad was out, so he was making the most of the opportunity.)

David also happened to be looking after the school gerbil called Dale – as in Chip 'n' Dale.

Dale was being given a bit of exercise out of his cage in David's bedroom.

For some reason best known to the reckless rodent – and contrary to everything they teach about road safety at his school – Dale decided to make a dash for it across the Scalextric track.

And you've guessed it – he got run over.

It might have been the Subaru. It might have been a Benetton. It could well have been

a Fur-arari. No one can really remember.

All David's mum can remember is hearing him shouting: "Mum, Mum quick!"

When she got there, the sight of blood made her panic. It was Dale.

He hadn't had his chips – but he'd had half his tail cut off.

The mum did her best to clean up the gerbil. If she'd been a dad, she'd have checked the car over first. (Congealed blood can affect the performance of a mean racing machine.)

In the end, Dale seemed none the worse, although he won't run across a Scalextric track again in a hurry.

But can you imagine the embarrassment of having to go into school after the holidays and say to the teacher: "Sorry – here's the gerbil back but I'm afraid it's only got half a tail because it got run over by a racing car on our Scalextric track."

The moral of this story for all you Scalextric fans out there – mainly dads, but kids as well – is this: When you're playing with your Scalextric, be prepared for anything. Absolutely anything.

And the moral for all you gerbils is this: "For goodness sake, look both ways and make sure the road is clear before you cross."

Things they don't say...

"Dad, don't waste your money taking us to McDonald's – it's just not nutritious enough."

One lump or two?

IT is a commonly held belief among women that men are hypochondriacs.

This, of course, is not true. It's just that men have a lower pain threshold than women. They also have more to worry about because they don't live as long as women.

This, however, doesn't stop women being generally intolerant and dismissive of men's aches, pains and very real fears.

Take, for example, the lump that grew on the crown of my head. It was the size of a pea to start with, but within a fortnight it was as big as a cherry tomato, though much harder.

At first, I thought it was something which would just disappear or burst. But it didn't and, naturally, I was beside myself with worry.

A cloud descended on me as I decided that I wasn't long for this world. I found it hard to concentrate, and sleep became a stranger as my imagination ran wild and the lump took on a sinister, ugly and chilling identity all of its own.

Finally, it all became too much to bear and I turned to my wife – my rock.

"Will you have a look at this lump on my head," I said, my voice low and quivering.

She foraged in my hair until she found the lump.

"Oh no," she said, quietly.

"What?" I asked, meekly.

"Oh no."

"What? Tell me."

"Oh my God."

"Look, just tell me what you think. Do you think I should be worried?"

"Good grief."

"WHAT?"

There was a long pause before she finally gave it to me straight: "I've just never realised before how thin your hair's going."

See what I mean? There's me – thinking I'm dying and looking for a bit of tender, loving care – and that's what I get.

And I'm not the only one. I was telling the story about my lumpy head to a female colleague and she brazenly announced that she'd done much the same thing to her husband.

By sheer coincidence, he'd had a lump growing on his bonce and it was preying on his mind as he and his wife went round the shops.

In the end, he couldn't stand the strain any longer and broke the news to his wife as she tried on a new outfit in a store fitting room.

"Linda, Linda," he whispered, "I've got a lump growing on my head. I'm really worried about it. Come and have a look."

She emerged from behind the curtain, stood before her panic-stricken husband, and said: "Well, what do you think? Is it me?"

"Linda!" protested the husband. "I've got a big lump growing out of my head and I'm really worried."

"Yes, yes," she replied, "but do you think I should buy it?"

I don't know what happened to *his* lump but I'm delighted to announce that mine turned out to be nothing sinister.

I finally plucked up the courage to go to see the doctor and within days it had been surgically removed at Darlington Memorial Hospital by the very same surgeon who performed my vasectomy. A top and tail job if ever there was one.

Thinking about it, my wife didn't take much notice of the pain I went through during my vasectomy either.

The things they say

"SOMETIMES I don't think you're cut out to be a dad." – Our five-year-old Jack after I said I was too busy to get him a drink.

Have a bit of patience

PARENTS never stop treating their offspring like children – even when those 'children' are middle-aged.

My dad clearly believes that I am still a seven-year-old, as opposed to a father-of-four hurtling towards 40. He also seems to think I'm a walking liability, not to say stupid.

"Don't let those bairns put their fingers in electric sockets. Don't let them hold lighted fireworks or play with boiling hot kettles."

Just a few of the instructions that regularly come my way.

When we're going off on holiday, it's even worse: "Mind those bairns don't fall off the ferry. Watch those kids in the pool. Don't let them eat anything that hasn't been cooked properly. Are you sure you'll be OK driving on the wrong side of the road?"

It drives me mad. In fact, on the eve of our two-week trip to Holland, I felt like saying: "Don't worry, Dad. I'll only let the older ones play with the propellers on the ferry; I promise to only leave them in the deep end on their own for an hour; I'll make extensive inquiries to find a restaurant that's got a strong reputation for food poisoning; and it'll be good experience for the three-year-old to see how he gets on driving on the right – he can't reach the pedals yet but he's a good steerer for his age."

We had an accident-free holiday. I had to phone home a few times to let Grandad know all was well, and that we hadn't let the kids try to swim the North Sea behind the ferry.

And, naturally, I phoned as soon as we got home to say we were back safe.

"*Are those bairns OK?*" he asked straight away.

"Yes." (Sigh.)

"*No problems?*"

"No." (Bigger sigh.)

"*Did you watch them?*"

"Yes." (Even bigger sigh.) How about you and Mum?" I asked.

"*Oh we're OK,*" he replied, matter-of-factly. "*We just had a bit of a fire.*"

The 'bit of a fire' turned out to be a brush with disaster. The smoke alarms upstairs had gone off while he was cutting the grass outside on his 75th birthday. He'd gone upstairs to find a bedroom smoke-logged and the bathroom ceiling in flames.

My mum came in from shopping as he was desperately trying to contain the fire by throwing water at it from a waste-paper bin – most of it landing back on him – having manfully dragged heavy ladders upstairs to open up the loft.

999 was dialled and two fire engines, with eight firemen, were there in four minutes to finish the job and heap praise on my dad for his efforts.

An electrical fault in the loft was diagnosed. They said it had probably been secretly smouldering for days and another few minutes would have resulted in the whole house being destroyed, along with next door.

The smoke alarms – fitted when the kids started to stay with Grandma and Grandad over occasional weekends – saved the day.

Had it happened at a different time, particularly at night, the alarms might easily have saved the lives of my parents and children.

The upstairs of the house is now being largely redecorated, although my dad is more concerned about the report in the paper which said: "Elderly couple survive blaze."

"Elderly? I'm not bloody elderly," the 75-year-old is said to have shouted.

The morals of this story? Have patience with those who worry about you only because they care. Worry about them back. And get smoke alarms fitted - **NOW!**

What do they really mean?

IT is a dilemma for dads everywhere – trying to work out what mums *really* mean.

Take last week for example. My wife actually said: "Don't worry about getting me anything for Valentine's Day – I know you love me and that's enough."

"Mmm," I thought to myself, "what does she really mean by that?"

She might have meant: "Don't worry about getting me anything for Valentine's Day – I know you love me and that's enough."

On the other hand, she could easily have meant: "If you don't get me anything for Valentine's Day, I'll never speak to you again, you can sleep in the spare room for a month, I'll take a pair of scissors to your best suits, and it'll be Pedigree Chum in your next chilli con carne."

You can see why it was a source of lost sleep. I like dogs but I'm not keen on Pedigree Chum.

In the middle of my week-long pondering of the problem, a fellow dad sent me something he'd coincidentally come across on the Internet.

It was headed "Women's English" – a translation of women's sayings for us men. Apparently, it is circulating among dads throughout the country.

Here are a few examples:

- "I'm sorry" – *"You'll be sorry"*
- "Do you love me?" – *"I'm going to ask for something very expensive"*
- "We need to talk" – *"I've got something to complain about"*
- "I'm not upset" – *"Of course I'm upset, you complete moron"*
- "It's your decision" – *"The correct decision should be obvious by now. Get it wrong and I'll make your life a misery"*
- "This kitchen's too small" – *"I want a new house"*
- "I'll be ready in a minute" – *"You might as well kick off your shoes, pour yourself a drink and find something to watch on TV for an hour"*

Call me stupid, call me reckless, but in the end I decided to call her bluff. After all, we've been married for 12 years this year and Valentine's Day is a needless expense.

The big day arrived and the only Valentine's cards in our house were addressed to the kids: Christopher, aged nine, didn't want to discuss it; Hannah, aged seven, just smiled and blushed; Jack, aged six, was so disgusted he went "yuk" and hid in the toilet; and Max, aged two, took no notice whatsoever.

It was only after an hour or so that the eldest, adopting a Sherlock Holmes persona, noticed that all four cards were in the same hand-writing. The finger of suspicion is pointing at Auntie Kim – her scribble on previous letters appears to fit, as does the Teesside postmark – but she's denying everything.

I admit to being a little disappointed that there was nothing romantic in the post for me, but relieved that (so far) there has been no bad reaction to my almighty gamble.

On the face of it, my wife is being very nice. She still seems to be talking to me, I've mostly stayed in the marital bed, and my suits are intact.

Mind you, that chilli con carne was a bit hard to swallow the other night...

And then there were seven

THERE weren't supposed to be any more babies. A family of six is quite enough for anyone. We even took drastic – exceptionally painful – measures to guarantee it couldn't happen.

And yet it *has* happened. We've got a new baby. She's tiny, cute, cuddly and everyone is smitten. We have become a family of seven.

Before any solicitors reach for the phone to help me sue the vasectomy clinic, I should make it clear that I'm only talking about a baby rabbit – but it's still another mouth to feed.

Hannah, aged seven, has been desperate for a pet but we've steered clear of them since the three goldfish – Bow, Arrow and Emma – died within weeks of coming home from the pet shop.

"Can I have a puppy? A kitten? A hamster? A gerbil? A rabbit? Please, please please."

We insisted she'd have to wait until she was old enough to look after it properly.

But then Brandy Berryman and Twinkle Berryman – bunnies belonging to some friends of ours – did what rabbits do naturally and we were offered one of their offspring.

The babies were born on January 1 – millennium bunnies – but we had to wait a while until they were ready to leave Twinkle's side and it was all kept a secret from Hannah, just in case anything went wrong.

They were finally ready to go to their various homes last weekend. Luckily, the kids were staying with Grandma so we had the chance to plan the surprise.

My mate Ken – an older, more experienced dad – kindly supplied the hutch: "Be prepared for tears," he warned, reflecting on the fact that dozens of beloved rabbits and guinea pigs have been buried in his garden over the years.

The hutch was squeezed into the corner of the garage and off we went to pick up baby bunny.

By the time the kids came home, the rabbit – white, with grey ears – was nicely settled in to her new home and we put on a video of the baby bunnies, taken shortly after they were born.

Hannah was immediately doe-eyed: "Aren't they lovely? Can I have a rabbit one day?"

"But where would we put it Hannah?" I asked.

"We could put it in a hutch in the corner of the garage – I'm sure there's room," she said.

"I don't think there is – come and show me."

We made our way to the garage and Hannah, still oblivious, pointed to the corner of the garage: "Look, we could put it there … oh, there's already a hutch there."

On cue, a little white nose poked round the corner. It's not very often you see children speechless, but Hannah looked up, with tears in her eyes, and couldn't say a word. It was one of those priceless moments that make being a dad the best job in the world.

Within an hour, we had 50 names written down – each being given marks out of ten. The boys fancied calling it Terminator, which didn't seem right for a baby girl rabbit. I suggested Cassie – short for casserole – but just got dirty looks. We managed to narrow it down to a shortlist of three, with Mulberry and Trixie the last to be discarded.

So welcome to the family, Jasmine Olivia Barron (Jazzy for short). Where will it all end?

Ask me anything, but not that

THOSE words "ask your father" have been a stock answer coming out of the mouths of mums for generations.

So facing embarrassing questions from children is part of the job description for us poor, hard-done-by dads.

It's not so long ago that our eldest – aged ten – nearly made me crash the car by asking: "Dad, does Father Christmas really exist?" quickly followed by "Dad, what's an orgasm?"

He'd heard the 'o' word being whispered at school and I did my best to give him a delicate explanation involving love and nice feelings.

A few weeks later, I was discussing the orgasm question with my childhood mate Colin, a father of two boys and a devoted Middlesbrough season ticket-holder.

"How would you have answered it, Col?" I asked.

"I'd have told the truth," he replied. "I'd have told him I couldn't remember."

He then went on to tell me how his youngest son Stephen had asked his own embarrassing question the week before:

"*Dad, can I ask you something?*"

"Course you can, son."

"*But it's a bit embarrassing, Dad.*"

"Oh I see. Don't worry. I'm your Dad, you can ask me anything."

"*But it's really embarrassing, Dad. I don't know if I can.*"

"Look, Stephen, don't be embarrassed, just ask me and I'll do my best to help."

"*Well, Dad, it's just that I was wondering. . .I was wondering. . .it's no good Dad, it's too embarrassing.*"

"STEPHEN, COME ON, JUST ASK!"

Stephen took a deep breath and went for it: "*Dad, is it alright if I support Man United?*"

His Dad moaned. And it had absolutely nothing to do with orgasms.

And then there were eight!

Four kids, a wife and a baby rabbit are enough for any dad to cope with.

But Jasmine the baby bunny had only been with us a week when it was suggested that she was lonely.

It was therefore decided – not that these things ever have much to do with me – that we should get her a companion.

So off we all went in the people carrier – all seven of us (including one in a box) – to find Jasmine a friend at Bunny Burrows, a rabbit sanctuary we'd heard of in Richmond.

There were plenty of rabbits to choose from, including four steel-grey youngsters with a pet mother and a wild father. (The mum had apparently escaped for an hour and found herself a bit of rough in a nearby field, the floosie.)

Eventually, we chose a small, white male with ginger lop ears, named him Aladdin, and brought him home.

Now, I'm sure you've spotted the potential flaw in this arrangement – Aladdin's a boy and Jasmine's a bunny girl. Mmm.

Yes, I know rabbits have a bit of a reputation, but we were only following the advice from Bunny Burrows: two boys will fight and two girls will fight, so for a long-term relationship, it's best to go with a boy and a girl.

We were assured that since they're still only babies, there's no danger of any hanky panky for a few months.

But it means that sooner rather than later, Aladdin is going to have to follow in my own terrified footsteps and have that operation beginning with 'v' that I still find it hard to speak about.

Having undergone the knife myself, I know it's not going to be easy for him. But I'll be with him all the way.

We'll do it together. And once it's over, we'll be able to look each other straight in the eye and have a bond – an understanding.

In the meantime, the relationship between him and her hasn't got off to a great start. We put them together in the run we've built in the garden and Jasmine quickly made it clear who's boss by chasing him round and round and nipping him on the bottom.

Things have improved a little but she still has a tendency to pick on him for no good reason so they're having to sleep in separate hutches.

If I could speak rabbit language, I'd be able to explain to him that it's a way of life he'll have to get used to – just as men the world over have had to.

And yet it must be particularly hard for rabbits to understand. After all, there's no washing-up to leave undone, there's no pub to be late home from, there's no toilet seat to leave up, and rabbits don't have any socks to leave under the bed.

All poor old Aladdin does is nibble on the grass and pick at the odd bit of cabbage, and he still gets it in the neck.

Rabbit, rabbit, rabbit...

And then there were seven again

L IFE can be cruel. And so can children… Jasmine, Hannah's baby rabbit, had been with us for three short weeks when she became ill.

She wasn't touching her food, and she'd stopped bouncing round the garden, exploring every leaf and petal, and tormenting the lop-eared Aladdin.

Instead, she hid under a lavender bush, hardly moving, and looking forlorn.

The vet diagnosed a blocked intestine and Jasmine stayed overnight to see if antibiotics and fluid injections would help. They didn't.

The next day, she had to endure the indignity of an enema to see if that would get anything moving. It didn't.

The day after, we gave our consent for an exploratory operation. A telephone call quickly followed, seeking permission to 'let her go' peacefully while she was under the anaesthetic.

And so little Jasmine succumbed to the same pet curse that robbed us of Bow, Arrow and Emma, the three goldfish. They'd only lasted three weeks too. Aladdin must be a very worried bunny – if I was him, I'd run rabbit run while I had the chance.

The news was broken to Hannah, aged seven, at the schoolgates, and two weeks of heartbreak have ensued. She's even been sleeping with a soft toy bunny for comfort.

Things weren't helped at school, where the naughtiest boy in class asked mockingly: "Is your rabbit dead yet?"

"Yes," replied Hannah, putting on a doe-eyed look.

The lad promptly started humming the funeral march, much to the amusement of other boys in the class.

It has to be said that there has been a certain degree of wallowing in the grief: "No, I need to have a proper cry over Jasmine when I get home," Hannah replied when it was suggested a few days later that a friend might like to come home for tea.

She's consoling herself with her vision of bunny heaven: "Rabbits can bounce around the clouds and there's a giant allotment where they can eat carrots all day and there's no foxes," she explained. (It's anyone's guess where dead foxes go.)

Jasmine was taken straight from the vet's to a pet crematorium in Durham so, unlike with the goldfish, there has been no funeral.

A wonky wooden cross memorial has, however, been cackhandedly created for the garden by her big brother.

And, in order to wallow in tragedy a bit more, Hannah wanted to write a poem of remembrance to take to school. Here's what she came up with (with just a little help from her Dad), so get your handkerchiefs out:

Goodbye Jasmine bunny,
I loved you very much,
I wish you didn't have to die,
And now it always makes me cry,
To see your empty hutch.

I know you've gone to heaven,
Where pets go if they're nice,
They hop around on clouds so white,
And slide down rainbows golden bright,
It's a bunny paradise.

So goodbye Jasmine bunny,
It's sad we had to part,
We were friends for just a little while,
But you made me happy – made me smile,
You'll be always in my heart.

"I don't think I'll ever get over this," she said, wiping away a tear. "When can we go and get another Jasmine?"

The great escape

SOMETIMES I wonder if it's all a bad dream...

There I was, at the wheel of the people-carrier – with one wife complaining about my driving, four kids asking "Are we there yet?" every two minutes, and a rabbit frantically scratching at the lid of his crisp box.

We were off to Bunny Burrows rabbit sanctuary at Richmond again to find a substitute Jasmine and ease the heartache. We'd been advised to bring Aladdin with us because bunnies apparently like to choose their own friends.

He was introduced first to a dark grey bunny girl called Liquorice but they didn't hit it off at all. Smartie, a white female with black markings similar to Jasmine's, came next and proved an altogether more successful partner.

And so it was that the newly-named Jasmine Smartie made the journey home in the people-carrier: One wife, four children, and two rabbits scratching at their boxes.

Since her arrival, Jasmine Smartie and Aladdin have been getting along very well – too well, in fact.

Whenever we put them in the same run, he'd try his luck. OK, so he got the wrong end most of the time, but you can't blame a rabbit for trying, can you?

We'd been assured that there couldn't be a baby boom just yet. Aladdin is still a youngster and Jasmine is a mature woman by comparison – the Anne Bancroft and Dustin Hoffman of the rabbit world – but you can't be too safe.

An anxious telephone call to Bunny Burrows, and a rapid calculation of dates, confirmed that there was nothing else for it: "He's not far off four months so it's probably best to get him sorted sooner rather than late," we were told.

I agreed to take him to the vet's. After all, I'd been through the same terrifying, agonising ordeal. I've been 'sorted' too and I'd been so frightened that the trolley rattled as I was wheeled to the operating theatre.

"Now look," I told Aladdin as I dropped him off on the way to work, "it's not very nice, and you'll be walking like John Wayne for a few weeks, but it's for the best."

There was a knowing look – an understanding – between us as the vet's assistant took him away in his box and told me to call around three o'clock that afternoon to see if he was ready.

I never got the chance to make that call. It was around midday and I was in the middle of an important meeting when the phone rang. It was the vet asking if I could pick up the rabbit early – they hadn't been able to carry out of the operation.

"Why not?" I enquired, instantly fearing that we'd lost another one under the knife.

"Because his testicles haven't dropped yet."

It wasn't an excuse I'd been able to offer up when I went for my little 'op', although I would have done if I thought I could have got away with it.

Aladdin has the look of a mightily relieved rabbit – but, ultimately, there can be no escape.

Bringing dads to book

WHEN my wife announced that she was forming a book club for mums in our village, I couldn't help but be impressed. They would read a book and get together monthly to discuss its merits or otherwise.

Great idea, I thought – educational, thought-provoking, challenging. But the truth about the book club has slowly dawned. It has precious little to do with books and lots to do with drinking wine and criticising dads.

Don't get me wrong – Shakespeare, Hardy, Lawrence and co. do get analysed. But not half as much as us ordinary blokes. Every chapter of our lives gets the Dickens of a going over. The main reason for getting together is to gauge how their husbands rate on: uselessness, thoughtlessness, stupidity, laziness, gullibility, and I dread to think what else.

Take the last meeting. The chosen book was called 'Men Are From Mars, Women Are From Venus' by John Gray – billed as "a practical guide to improving communication and getting what you want in your relationships". Spot the flaw? The author's a man – how can a man know anything about getting what you want in relationships?

Anyway, the book review was barely five minutes old, and only four bottles of wine had been drunk, before someone asked the question upon which the entire future of British literature may depend: "How does your husband hang out the washing?"

I doubt whether it's a question which has ever come up at Booker Prize judging sessions. Who knows, perhaps the mummies thought Shakespeare had a clothes horse in mind when Richard the Third declared: "A horse, a horse, my Kingdom for a horse."

Anyway, hanging washing is one of the skills upon which us hubbies are judged. Here's the book club's analysis of the various categories:

1. **WIDE-EYED AND PEGLESS:** Takes washing out of machine, slings it over shoulder and flings each item over line any old way. Never uses pegs. Relies on a calm day to keep washing in place until dry. (Wife wishes he just didn't bother.)

2. **PEGGY IN THE MIDDLE:** Takes washing from machine, slings it over shoulder, (see a common denominator emerging?) picks up peg box/bag and drapes washing over line, securing each item with one central peg.

3. **PEG, STEAL OR BORROW:** Takes washing from machine, puts it in basket (ah, a new man!), picks up peg box/bag overflowing with pegs, and proceeds to line. (So far, so good.) Carefully hangs washing correctly but main characteristic is that he will do anything to use as few pegs as possible and is therefore obsessed with peg-sharing. Despite having many more pegs than necessary, attaches two garments with one peg. (Wife hates this. Cannot see why all items are denied their own, exclusive pegs. However, in his defence, this man also irons.)

4. **ALL PEGGED OUT:** Too tired after work to be bothered.

5. **PEG IGNORANT:** Doesn't think it's a man's job.

6. **PEGS MIGHT FLY:** It just never occurs to him.

As Shakespeare once said (A Midsummer Night's Dream – Act 1 Scene 1): "The course of true love never did run smooth."

An idiots' guide

"TAKE washing out of machine and place in basket. Remember to flick each garment (men don't flick) to reduce creasing, and hang, usually upside down, with one peg in each corner. Sometimes, depending on garment, peg it under arms to prevent stretching. When dry, washing should be removed from line and folded carefully...oh forget it. It's all very technical and therefore beyond most men." – **By my wife.**

DARLINGTON
BOROUGH COUNCIL

Darlington Local Authority Nursery Schools

ALBERT HILL NURSERY SCHOOL
Prescott Street
Darlington DL1 2ND
(01325) 380818
Headteacher
Mrs C D Billington

parent and toddler group
starting after Easter '01

BOROUGH ROAD NURSERY SCHOOL
Borough Road
Darlington DL1 1SG
(01325) 380785

Headteacher
Mrs L Millar

playgroup to start for nursery
children in September '01

CORPORATION ROAD NURSERY CENTRE
Corporation Road
Darlington
(01325) 244940

Headteacher
Mrs C Dawson

childcare facility
on premises

All six nursery schools offer:

- Highly qualified, committed and professional staff who work together to give the best possible start to your child's education

- Carefully planned provision with high quality learning resources

- Purposeful play in a caring, safe and exciting environment that builds on learning at home

- A smooth transition from home to school

- Identification of individual learning needs and progression towards the Early Learning Goals

- Quality ensured by inspections to the rigorous standards set by Ofsted

EASTBOURNE NURSERY SCHOOL
Belgrave Street
Darlington
DL1 4AP
(01325) 380825

Headteacher
Mrs P Beavis

HEATHFIELD NURSERY SCHOOL
The Broadway
Darlington
DL1 1EJ
(01325) 380827

Acting Headteacher
Mrs S Horner

GEORGE DENT NURSERY SCHOOL
Elms Road
Darlington
DL3 7PY
(01325) 380802

Headteacher
Mrs P Pennington

Cut off in his prime

ULTIMATELY, there could be no escape from the dreaded knife.

Aladdin, the amorous male rabbit, had got away with it once – by a hare's breadth, so to speak – because the vet discovered his testicles hadn't dropped.

But, two months on, the time had come for him to face up to the same harrowing fate that many of us dads have had to endure.

It had to be done. Aladdin and Jasmine could never be together otherwise. They'd have to stay in separate hutches – her up top and him in the basement.

My wife took him to the vet's this time – the memories were too painful for me.

The vet turned Aladdin over and searched for his bits while he lolled back and rolled his eyes – a bit like me.

"There's one," she declared. "And there's the other – that's all we need."

I thought about him all day at work. My mind flashed sympathetically back to those dark days when I could hardly walk.

But women don't have much sympathy when it comes to such delicate matters – a fact underlined when I telephoned home for a condition check:

"Has he been done?" I asked.

"Yes, he's home," said my wife.

"How is he?" I enquired.

"Fine," she replied.

"Is he distressed?" I wondered.

"Oh for goodness sake – it's only a minor operation," she snapped.

ONLY A MINOR OPERATION! That's mums all over isn't it? One of us males has his manhood severed and they think it's nothing important. It's an outrage.

Suppressing my anger, I calmly asked if he'd require any more treatment.

"He's got to go for a check-up on Saturday and he mustn't get sawdust in his stitches."

It was a piece of advice I'd never had. Mind you, I don't suppose they told Aladdin to wear loose underpants for a fortnight.

"At least they'll be able to move in together now," I suggested.

Oh no they wouldn't, she informed me. They'd have to be kept apart for another six weeks to be absolutely sure.

Poor Aladdin. He must be one confused little bunny. They take a scalpel to his crown jewels and he still can't be with the one he loves.

We have to go on taking steps to ensure they never get it together. When one is having a romp round the garden, the other has to stay locked up in its run.

A week after Aladdin's major surgery, I was left in charge of the two older children and two rabbits while mum and the two little ones went to see Noddy at the theatre.

It was sunny so Jasmine was bouncing round the garden, Aladdin was in the run, the kids were watching videos, and I had my feet up on the patio, reading the paper.

I don't know what made me look up but it was a sight that filled me with horror. There they were – TOGETHER! Somehow, Aladdin had escaped and made a beeline for his bunny girl.

Did they have time to do *it*? Could Jasmine be pregnant? Will my wife take a sharp knife to my already scarred nether regions?

The answer to all of these questions is that I simply don't know ... but I am a very worried daddy.

Bunny Burrows...

CAN you give a bunny a good home? Call John and Gwen Butler at Bunny Burrows rabbit sanctuary in Richmond, North Yorkshire, on (01748) 824788. They've got more rabbits than they know what to do with, and Gwen's so busy looking after the bunnies that poor old John doesn't get a look in.

With this ring...

ULTIMATUMS come thick and fast when you're a dad, which is why we're under such intense pressure.

My wife has given me three for the year 2000 – warning that she'll seek a younger model if I fail.

Ultimatum number one – I must not lose my wedding ring again. I lost my first ring two years ago and it took ages for her to buy me a replacement. Like the original, it's engraved with our initials and anniversary date. I'm so terrified that I've vowed never to take it off.

Ultimatum number two was a shock: "You have to put the salt and vinegar back in the middle of the table after using them."

Sorry?

"You always keep them next to your own plate. It gets on my nerves."

Oh. It's only taken 12 years for my spices vice to be revealed.

The third ultimatum has been eating away at our marriage since day one: The nail-biting must stop. So far so good – I haven't bitten them for four months. Mind you, I have gone from chewing 20 pen tops a day to 30.

And I've tried really hard at meal-times. I reach over, grab the salt, sprinkle some on my food, then concentrate until it's back where it belongs – exactly in the middle of the table. An inch either way could spell disaster. Same goes for the vinegar.

But it's my ring which poses the biggest threat, and that's why the weekend was so stressful. I'd taken my little boy for his Sunday morning swimming lesson and I decided to do a few lengths myself.

Half way up my first length, my arm came over in a perfect crawl ...and my ring slipped off my wet finger, spun into an arc and splashed into the deep end.

Lifeguards appeared from everywhere, which isn't surprising because there was a grown man screaming inexplicably in the middle of the pool.

"I've lost my ring," I shouted and – concluding that no lives were in danger – they went away. Poor judgement – my life had never been in greater danger.

Heart thumping so hard it was making little splashes, I swam around, desperately looking for a glint of gold. Nothing.

I couldn't dive under because of my contact lenses. I tried asking a young couple for help but – despite the warning signs – they were too busy indulging in a spot of heavy petting to listen. The only other swimmer was an old man who resembled Jacques Cousteau but could barely doggy-paddle, let alone dive to the bottom in search of lost treasure.

Suddenly, hope emerged from the changing room – a little boy wearing goggles.

"'Scuse me son, I need those," I cried, snatching them off his head in a mad panic.

The goggles were so tight that the lack of blood to my head made me dizzy as I floated up and down. Still nothing.

Maybe it had fallen down a drain? Or got caught between the old man's toes? I considered grabbing his leg and lifting him upside down but I already felt guilty about mugging the boy.

I was about to pass out from the lack of blood when I saw it. On the bottom, nowhere near where I thought it had landed, was my precious ring.

I took a deep breath, dived down, and grabbed it first time. The lifeguards were woken up again, this time by a strange man whooping for joy.

I've never felt so relieved. Mind you, I came very close to biting my nails again.

The things they say...

THERE is a popular advert on TV for a well-known brand of lager which involves lots of people ringing each other and shouting "What's up?" down the phone.

"What's up?" has evolved into a kind of "Whazzar?" You know the one. Well, a working mum, who wishes to remain anonymous but is quite a public figure in Darlington, has adopted "Whazzar?" as a regular greeting to her son.

They ring each other and shout "Whazzar?" down the phone. Strange, I know, but that's modern parenthood.

Anyway, the mum was in the queue for the till at a town centre store when her mobile telephone rang: "Whazzar?" shouted her son.

The mum, conscious of all the people near her, cupped her hand round the phone and replied softly: "Whazzar?"

"Mum, I can't hear you – whazzar?" the boy shouted again.

"Whazzar?" the mum replied a little louder.

"Mum, I still can't hear you – whazzar?"

"Whazzar," she replied a little louder again.

"Mum, I still can't hear you – whazzar?"

This went on for a few more minutes before the red-faced mum found herself yelling **"WHAZZAR!"** down the phone at the top of her voice while lots of shoppers looked on incredulously.

I WAS delighted to talk at a fund-raising evening at Bishop Auckland Methodist Church and Margaret Nicholson was kind enough to pass on this gem from her grandson Oliver, aged four: "Daddy, why do Grandma and Grandad wobble?"

A question of honesty

IT is a police scandal which will reverberate around the corridors of power for years to come.

The traditional ideals of fairness and honesty, symbolised by good old Dixon of Dock Green, have been thrown in the gutter. How could it have come to this .. ?

The call which was to expose this particular outrage was made to our home at 9pm, just as the kids were settling down to sleep.

"Quick, quick – I haven't got much time," gushed the caller.

He was breathless. He was desperate. He was clearly in no mood for messing about. It was Uncle John, a uniformed officer with Cleveland Police, based at Hartlepool.

"This is important – who runs the Post Office in Postman Pat?" he demanded to know.

"Oh," said my wife, somewhat startled. "I think it was Mrs Goggins – hold on."

I'm sure I would have stopped to ask why he wanted to know, but she ran upstairs to check with our eldest.

"Christopher, Uncle John's on the phone. He wants to know who ran the Post Office in Postman Pat," she said.

Christopher sat up in bed, his brow creased in thought: "Mrs C...Mrs Cog...Mrs Goggins!"

"Good – that's what I thought," she replied before running back downstairs.

"It *is* Mrs Goggins," she told Uncle John.

"Right – who were the parents in 101 Dalmatians?" he barked.

"Dogs or humans?" she asked.

"Dogs, the dogs – quick, I'm running out of money."

"Perdita and Pongo," came the answer.

"Great, that's great. Gotta go," he snapped, and then he was gone.

He was a good deal calmer when he rang back 24 hours later: "Sorry about last night, I was in a quiz. Thanks for your help, it moved us up from last to fourth place."

Apart from making her feel that she was only good for answering questions about children's videos, when she has, in fact, been known to get one or two right on University Challenge, it made my wife wonder about the integrity of our guardians of what's right and wrong.

"Are you allowed to use a phone during the quiz?" she asked, not unreasonably.

"You wouldn't believe it," he said. "It was a quiz in the police social club and they were all using mobile phones to get the answers."

In order words, the police officers of Hartlepool were shamelessly cheating.

And if you ask me, they should all be brought in for questioning ...

TEN THINGS HARTLEPOOL POLICE OFFICERS SHOULD KNOW (Because it might save their integrity...and their phone bills):

1. Simba's father in the Lion King is called Mufasa.

2. The Seven Dwarfs are called Doc, Happy, Grumpy, Sleepy, Sneezy, Bashful and Dopey.

3. Toy Story star Woody is a cowboy.

4. The farmer in Babe is called Farmer Hoggett.

5. Thomas The Tank Engine lives on the island of Sodor.

6. Fireman Sam's engine is called Jupiter.

7. Bambi's friend Thumper is a rabbit.

8. It's a magic feather which enables Dumbo to fly.

9. Winnie the Pooh's adventures take place in the Hundred Acre Wood.

10. The policeman in Noddy is called PC Plod – **AND HE SAYS IT'S VERY, VERY NAUGHTY TO CHEAT!**

Let the train increase the strain

CHILDREN have a habit of saying the wrong thing at the wrong time...

"Dad, you're going bald." – Jack, aged six, just as I was convincing myself in front of the mirror that it wasn't really a bald patch, just a bad haircut.

"Mum, can I come and sleep in your bed?" – Max, aged three, on the night of our 12th anniversary, just as the flame of romance was starting to grow from a flicker to an Olympic torch.

"Look, that man's got big boobies, hasn't he Daddy." – Hannah, when she was three, as a fat man joined us in the jacuzzi at a local health club.

But of all the wrong things they've said at the wrong time, nothing has pained me quite as much as the words which greeted me as I stepped through the door after my ill-fated business trip to Birmingham.

I'd travelled to the Midlands the night before. I'd arrived safely in my hotel and even had time for a relaxing swim and 15 minutes in the jacuzzi with two men, neither of whom had particularly big boobies.

The business was duly completed the next morning and I set off on the homeward journey, eager to be back reasonably early because it was our eldest's 10th birthday.

At Birmingham railway station, the 12.45pm Virgin service to Darlington had been delayed by a line blockage at Chesterfield.

I waited the best part of an hour before the train finally arrived and I was grateful to settle into my first-class seat and empty my briefcase onto the table so I could work on the journey.

The train didn't move. Then a scratchy tannoy message crackled through the carriage: "This train is being converted into the Aberdeen service, so please get off." Or words to that effect.

I gathered up my papers and got off. We then waited at least another hour on the platform – with precious little information – for another promised train to arrive.

It never came. Another scratchy message: "Would passengers travelling to York and Darlington please make their way to the front of the station where a bus will take them to York." Or words to that effect.

A groan echoed along the platform but we did as we were told. At the front of the station, I looked up and down for a luxury coach but there was only a grubby old double-decker.

Oh my God, our bus *was* the double-decker. I looked around for Jeremy Beadle but he was nowhere to be seen.

This was no ordinary double-decker. It was a smelly, cold, double-decker that appeared unable to go faster than three miles an hour up the slightest incline. I swear we were overtaken by a hedgehog walking up the hard-shoulder of the A1 somewhere near Pontefract.

Apart from a 15-minute break for a sandwich and a wee, we were crammed on that bus for the best part of four hours. Anyone with long legs, like me, had to travel with their knees on their chins and I happened to be sat next to a poor mum struggling to keep her grizzly two-year-old amused. Talk about cruelty to animals...

If I'd bumped into Richard Branson, I'd have said something like: "Excuse me Mr Branson, ever so sorry to trouble you, but is it any wonder your balloon never makes it round the world when you can't even get people from Birmingham to Darlington without turning them into physical and emotional wrecks?"

By the time we reached York, I was so stiff I could only hobble off the bus. The half-hour wait for a train connection to Darlington sent the blood pressure beyond danger point and it was past 8.30pm by the time I finally staggered through the door.

That's when the birthday boy said it:

"Hi Dad – had a good trip?"

No business like show business

BACK to the rabbits…It was the week of the village fete. We go every year, but this time it was special.

There were stalls, bouncy castles, miniature train rides and a line dancing display among the attractions.

But it was the pet competition which caught the eye when a leaflet about the fete arrived at our house – especially the category entitled "Cutest Rabbit In Show".

Jasmine and Aladdin had, as you know, become firmly established as part of the family, although the novelty had admittedly worn off somewhat.

In fact, we'd reached the point at which that familiar mums' grumble was to be heard regularly: "If it wasn't for me, those rabbits would starve. Not one of you pays them any attention. You just don't care."

This was, of course, directed not only at the four children but me as well.

She'd even issued an ultimatum: "If you don't start looking after them properly, they'll have to go."

She didn't mean it, of course. It's just what mums say. My mum used to say exactly the same thing about my rabbit when I was little but she never got rid of him.

Thankfully, the news of the "Cutest Rabbit In Show" competition inspired renewed interest in Jasmine and Aladdin.

On the morning of the fete, Hannah, aged eight, was up early to get them ready. Jasmine got stage fright, jumped free from her hutch and refused to be caught. She's a little madam but it was her loss.

Aladdin's cuter anyway. He's snowy white with ginger lop ears. Let's just say we were hopeful of victory.

He had his coat brushed lots of times and his tail was nicely fluffed up before he was placed

carefully in a cardboard box for the short drive to the fete.

The tension mounted inside the show tent. Our heartbeats quickened as the stern-faced, white-coated judge walked towards us.

He picked up Aladdin and held him by the ears before unceremoniously turning him onto his back. Naturally, we felt obliged to tell him about the little operation he'd had to stop Jasmine getting pregnant, just in case it had a bearing on the result.

The judge remained silent. Curiously, he pulled Aladdin's top lip back and muttered something about crooked front teeth.

Our hearts sank. How important would crooked front teeth prove to be in a cute bunny contest? Was it our fault? Were our carrots too hard? Should we have made him wear a brace?

The judge put Aladdin back down, took a step back and assessed him again. Still not a murmur.

Finally, he broke his silence: "What do you feed him on?"

"Rabbit food," replied Hannah.

Stupid man. What did he think we fed him on – spaghetti bolognaise?

The judging seemed to take ages. The tension inside the tent became almost unbearable. Then the announcement came:

"And the silver cup for the cutest rabbit in show goes to – **ALADDIN**."

Yes! He'd done it. Oh joy of joys. Hannah stepped forward proudly to accept the silver cup. It now has pride of place in her bedroom next to her Worker of the Week certificate.

The record books will show that Aladdin was the cutest bunny in show. The fact that he was the only rabbit entered matters not one jot.

Chips off the old block

THE ageing process is getting me down. For a start, I've started growing little tufts of hair on my back and in my ears.

I've started listening to Radio 2 – even Terry Wogan – and I can't stand to be in the same room when my daughter's playing her music.

"It's just a noise," I find myself shouting, just like my dad used to during my years devoted to Top of the Pops.

I thought the sense of rapid ageing couldn't get any worse than when me and five other dads embarked on a golfing weekend to Dublin recently.

In a desperate search for our lost youth, we found ourselves in a nightclub. In fact, I think it was one of those rave clubs – the nearest thing to hell I could imagine.

It was too hot to breathe, so packed you couldn't move, the music was so loud that you couldn't talk to anyone, and the drinks were so expensive that I had to stay thirsty.

To cap it all, I ended up being asked to dance by a bloke I'd never seen before in my life.

Having politely declined, I looked around, realised I was old enough to have fathered everyone else in sight, and began inching towards the door.

Oh yes, the Dublin experience was bad. But the passing of time really hit me when I got back home and took the kids over to Grandma's house.

She'd promised to cook them lunch, but there was a problem: "Oh no, I've run out of chips," she cried, shortly after our arrival.

Looks of horror spread across the faces of our hungry foursome. No chips – the world had come to an end. How could life possibly go on?

To children, a house without chips is as horrific as a rave club to a dad hurtling towards 40.

But grandmas are nothing if not resourceful: "Don't worry, it won't take me long to peel a few spuds," she declared.

The looks of horror turned to looks of wonder: "What are you going to do with that?" asked six-year-old Jack, pointing at a potato in her hand.

"I'm going to make some chips," replied Grandma.

Jack laughed. "But it's round and hard."

Grandma got on with the job in hand. Jack couldn't believe what he was seeing.

"Quick, quick," he shouted to the others, "Grandma's making chips out of real potatoes."

"Wow," said Christopher, aged ten, as they gathered in the kitchen, watching her cut the real potatoes into chip shapes, and pour them into boiling oil. "That's amazing."

She wasn't splitting the atom. She wasn't creating a masterful piece of art. She wasn't even doing magic. She was just making chips – out of real potatoes.

I watched in wonderment too – that I am in the middle of raising children who've never seen chips that didn't come out of a packet.

They even tasted good: "These are really nice – even better than real chips," said Jack.

The things they say...

A MUM called Hilary was endeavouring to carry some washing down the stairs with one-year-old Libby sitting in the basket.

Tom, aged seven, decided to sit on the stairs to put his socks on.

"Tom, don't sit there – I'll trip over the top of you, and Libby and I will fall to the bottom," said Hilary.

"Don't worry," he replied in a very serious voice, "we'll just call Claims Direct –. I've seen an advert on the telly and we'll get some money if you fall."

Ten minutes later, Tom appeared in the kitchen.

"I've been thinking," he said, "if there was a Claims Direct for kids, we could be millionaires."

"WHY do we send the Queen plums?" Janet Paterson, of Dalton, near Darlington, asked her mum when she was a little girl.

"Why on earth do you ask that?" replied her mum.

"Because," answered Janet, " when we're singing the national anthem, we say 'Send her Victorias'".

TAMARA, a friend's little girl, was sat with her mum, watching the final episode of Inspector Morse.

A murdered body was being bundled into the boot of a car.

"Eee, they shouldn't be doing that, should they mum?" said Tamara. "They'll never be able to fit the shopping in."

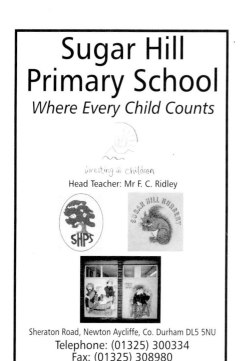

A carry-on camping

CAMPING never appealed, even when I was little. Too many creepy crawlies, too cold, too wet.

As a grown-up, it is considerably less attractive...

When our first-born announced he wanted a camping party for his tenth birthday, all eyes were on me. (Equality is all very well unless it involves any level of discomfort.)

After weeks of disorganisation, I found myself erecting a borrowed tent in the garden. Thankfully, I had the help of a brother-in-law with 20 years experience in the Army, otherwise I'd still be erecting it now.

The birthday boy had invited two pals to join the adventure. He'd also agreed, reluctantly, that his little brother could camp out too.

Between them, they'd made a long list of essentials: Pillows, sleeping-bags, torches, spare batteries, saucepan, beans, sausages, marshmallows, giant bar of chocolate, Bart Simpson book, bug-repellent, drinks, Game-Boys, cake, midnight snacks, junk food, more junk food, even more junk food, mugs, warm clothes, pyjamas, waterproofs, plastic bags, newspaper, rope, saftey pins, Sellotape, scissors, and – get this one – an old tin bucket for 'emergency wees' in the night.

Once the tent was up, the next task was to build a campfire to cook the grub. Again with Army advice, a turf was cut out of the garden, cooking foil laid in the hole, barbecue charcoal poured in, and fire-lighters lit. Before long, it had a healthy glow in the descending gloom.

That's when the rain started. Luckily, we had a large Army-issue umbrella on hand to cover the fire. The sausages cooked a treat, the beans warmed nicely, the eggs fried enthusiastically, and the raindrops slithered off the umbrella and trickled down my back.

Naturally, I'd have slept in the tent with the kids if it hadn't been for my bad back (I'd been in agony all day and, no, it wasn't psychosomatic, whatever my wife says about 'excuses, excuses'). Instead, I slept within earshot, on cushions on the lounge floor, with the patio doors open. My wife had thoughtfully popped her head in to say: "I'm just going up to my nice, warm, soft, very big bed now."

I hardly slept a wink. I listened to the chatter drifting from the tent. I watched the torches flashing on and off like a mini disco.

1.27am: Little brother stumbled noisily over a guyrope and fell into the – mercifully, still empty – emergency wee bucket.

2.25am: One of the pals wandered over to ask if everyone in the house was asleep. "Sadly not," I replied.

2.54am: Birthday boy emerged to ask for a drink, or was it reassurance?

3.15am: Pal number two came across to ask "Is it midnight yet?"

And all the time my back ached. I woke at 4.30am to find birthday boy peering at me: "Dad, emergency – there's a wasp and a red ant in the tent."

The others were all standing in the garden and it was still raining. My back wouldn't bend far enough for me to put my shoes on so I splodged barefoot across the sodden grass.

"They won't hurt," I promised.

"But Dad, we can't sleep with them in there. We'll get stung," birthday boy replied.

"Why not call it a night and come into the house?" I suggested, hopefully.

Birthday boy hesitated before saying: "No Dad, I don't want to be a quitter."

"You're not a quitter. It's nearly five o'clock – you've done really well," I insisted.

They needed no further persuasion. All four had rushed past me into the house and were leaping into whatever bed they could find before I had time to say 'Survival Special'.

"Thank God that's over," I thought, as I found the bottom bunk going spare.

Outside, a waking bird uttered a cry that sounded suspiciously like mocking laughter.

My back didn't half ache.

Fatherhood

If I was just an ordinary man,
And I ran down the sand,
Skimmers leaving my hand,
To bounce through the sea,
Trousers rolled to my knees,
Toes kissed by the tide,
Butterflies dancing inside,
Building castles and moats,
Racing driftwood as boats,
They would say I was mad,
But I'm not – I'm a dad

And that means I can,
As an extraordinary man,
Become Peter Pan,
Or dress up as Santa,
Then gallop and canter,
When I'm being a horse,
Wild Bill Hickok's of course,
Wearing holes in my jeans,
Before fishfingers and beans,
Oh what fun I've had,
Just by being a dad.

There's no time to rest,
Kicking footballs I'm blessed,
With the skills of George Best,
And at pantos I shout,
"He's behind you – watch out"
I fight dragons and beasts,
Prepare midnight feasts,
Fly kites in the breeze,
Aim at conkers in trees,
I can drive bumper cars,
Camp out under stars,
Go fishing in streams,
Live out all of my dreams,
The magic of being a dad,
Makes me more happy than sad,
Eases all growing pains,
Gives me childhood again...